Scripture and Imagination

Scripture and Imagination

THE EMPOWERING OF FAITH

WILLIAM BEAVEN ABERNETHY
and
PHILIP JOSEPH MAYHER

Introduction by
MARIA HARRIS

The Pilgrim Press New York

All scripture quotations, unless otherwise indicated, are from the Revised Standard Version of the Bible, copyrighted 1946, 1952, © 1971, 1973, by the Division of Christian Education of the National Council of Churches of Christ in the United States of America, and are used by permission.

Library of Congress Cataloging-in-Publication Data

Abernethy, William Beaven, 1939–
    Scripture and imagination: the empowering of faith /
William Beaven Abernethy and Philip Joseph Mayher:
introduction by Maria Harris.

    Bibliography: p. 121
    ISBN 0-8298-0794-2
    1. Church group work.   2. Christian education of adults.
I. Mayher, Philip Joseph.   II. Title.
BV652.2A24   1988
268'.434—dc19   88-21637
                                                        CIP

The Pilgrim Press, 132 West 31 Street, New York, NY 10001

We dedicate this book to

Our wives—Ann and Cindy
Our children—Mark, Sarah, Jonathan, and Laura
Aaron and Jessamyn

And We Offer Our Gratitude to

The Members of Faith Empowering Groups
The Wellesley Congregational Church (United Church of Christ)
Wellesley, Massachusetts

And to our doctoral committee at
Andover Newton Theological School

The Rev. Richard Broholm,
Dr. Gabriel Fackre,
Dr. Maria Harris,
and Dr. George Sinclair

And we acknowledge with appreciation
the editorial assistance of

Deborah Rose

Contents

Preface

This is the story of faith empowering groups. Such an ambitious-sounding name designates a six-step adult education method, in use since 1980, through which participants seek to grow in their faith by availing themselves of each other, God's Word, and the imaginative movement of the Spirit in their lives. Our purpose here is to describe this process in detail. Yet more importantly, we want to testify to the power of biblical faith, enlivened through imagination and an authentic concern for persons wanting to renew their faith journeys.

We share this story on the assumption that we are all wanderers in time, struggling for the clues and the cues that might ignite our encounter with God or deepen our contact with each other as a next step in the faith journey. Out of the life of many different faith empowering groups, we hope to tell a tale of support for wanderers, to disclose yet one more hearth of the Spirit to warm searching fingers, and to illumine our connectedness with the All that is Holy.

What follows in chapter one are some narrative recollections from actual faith empowering group sessions to help you understand on a feeling level what we are about. Chapter two summarizes the process used in those groups, and the next six chapters describe that process in "how to do it" detail, along with some of the rationale behind these groups. After a discussion in chapter nine of the preparation that goes on before a faith empowering session, we move to a chapter which offers testimony from participants as they reflect upon their experiences, as well as the theoretical understanding of faith upon which the method is based.

Chapter eleven describes alternative settings where the model may be used, as well as alternative formats for special needs. Chapter twelve gives some specific information for those seeking to start a faith empowering program. In the final chapter, we share some sample guided meditations from many authors. These meditations may give incentive to those ready to try their own hand at such creative expressions, or may serve as an actual resource for use in your own faith empowerment. While they stand as *our* last words in this book, our deeper conviction has become that *God's* own authoring Spirit has been present throughout.

God's Spirit, we believe, is not unlike that relentless widow coming before the judge (Luke 18:1–8), demanding a hearing, ready to testify. And we who encounter that relentless widow—we have wanted to move beyond our sometimes judging, occasionally jaded, often overstressed sensibilities, and listen. We have sought to listen to each other, and to listen to God's voice. We have desired to be faithful to the question Jesus posed at the end of that Lukan parable: "Nevertheless, when the Son of man comes, will he find faith on earth?"

Introduction

I cannot pretend to be an objective, dispassionate reader of *Scripture and Imagination*. I have known Joe Mayher and Bill Abernethy for too long, observed their graceful and graced commitment to ministry too carefully, and met too many people who have been affected by that ministry to write a "distanced" or non-involved introduction. Instead, therefore, allow me to claim the insight and understanding that come from continuing awareness, direct experience, and confirmed judgment. For I think I have a sense of what they are up to here, having seen the work of faith empowerment when it was being birthed, and having watched it grow through the years. And I think I can present at least one point of view on how it stands now, grown as it has into maturity and integrity.

Integrity. That is, in my judgment, the key word. This is a work of integrity. In the fundamental meaning of that word, this is a work of *wholeness*, of unity and completeness. As I found myself reading and then centering on this theme of integrity/wholeness as my basic response, I realized why that was the symbol I wanted to choose in presenting the work to a larger audience. For I realized the integrity/wholeness is expressed in the book in at least the following ways.

First, the book is co-written. It has the unity that comes from the human conversation of two partners who have worked through their material to such a degree that no seams appear in the text, no boundaries assert a division of labor. Instead, there is an integrating of labor, an interplay of ideas, synergistically richer for having been filtered through two creative spirits rather than one.

Even more, however, the co-authors have at least implicitly made additional co-authors of the persons in the communities with whom they have worked in faith empowerment groups. Their use of the ideas and experiences—as well as the insights—of those who have participated in this work, is beautifully incorporated into the work as a whole. Because of this, the reading becomes the story of a body of people, a communion of living saints, and not the story of what the two co-authors did. And as this happens, it becomes possible for us the readers to find ourselves imaginatively participants with them in the story recorded here.

The book is not only written in a way that *demonstrates* wholeness, however. For at other levels the book is *about* wholeness and the ways to achieve it—especially in the ways that people come to know themselves and the Creative Spirit, and the ways people are led to integrate their logical, rational and intellectural powers with those which are intuitive, symbolic and metaphoric. If there is any core meaning of the term "imagination," it lies in this arena. Imagination is about integrity in human knowing, about wholeness, about our capacity to bring all our ways of framing experience into a kind of unity. Imagination is the power each of us possessess to make into one—Kant's *einbildungskraft*—the power of shaping into a whole. Or in the words of William Lynch, it is "all the faculties of human beings, all our resources, not only our seeing and hearing and touching, but also our history, our education, our feelings, our wishes, our love, hate, faith and unfaith, insofar as they go into the making of our image of the world." The beauty of this book is that it shows us how to do this, by offering a process through which we might achieve such wholeness.

And then it is also an integrating of horizons. One of the key elements you will discover as you read is the notion of horizon in biblical, religious, and personal life. The book gives us a process whereby we might address horizon, the "range of vision that includes everything that can be seen from a particular vantage point," (Gadamer) especially our own personal horizon in relation to biblical horizon. Their illustration of how distance and fusion make responsible understanding of the relation between these horizons is not only intelligent and compelling, it is also unique in theological and religious education. If for no other reason (although there are others), the book is needed because it enables us to do this.

And it enables us to do this in large part because of the way it is written. For one thing it is one of the most beautifully *written* books I have come across in a long time: absolutely jargon-free; lucid, often lyrical in its prose. But it is also written in an organic, human way. Although the order is clear—there *are* six steps in the process—the steps are not presented as if they were on a staircase or a ladder. Instead they are presented as steps in a dance, and in the reading we find ourselves circling back, repeating rhythmically, and understanding that this way of proceeding feels right to us because it is the rhythm of our human being, not the rhythm of the machine.

How do they do all this? How do they accomplish it? As you read you will come to your own conclusions about these questions, but I believe three are critical.

First, the authors tell this story and offer this process through careful, yet unobtrusive scholarship. When they cite someone—Gadamer, or Ricoeur, or Parks or Dr. Seuss—the impression they give is that the work of this person has been assimilated into the book as a whole. This is especially true of the biblical scholarship and the educational scholarship they bring to bear on the imaginative process described. I cannot think of one citation offered simply to "pad" or as an exercise in namedropping. Instead, the scholarship is integral to the book, extraordinary in its range, and invaluable to the reader wanting to go further. Put another way, besides being strong in the heart, the book is strong in the head.

A second way they work their wisdom is through giving a central role to experience. They work with participants' human lives, convinced as are the scriptures themselves, that this is where the Holy One is found; and that God has not retired from the world leaving divine truths behind. Instead, God is still with us in the ordinariness of our days. They bring this rich understanding of experience to bear in making the biblical connections, offering many arresting and even charming interpretations. I had never realized the humanity of Jesus in quite the way I did while reading a description of the story of the paralytic lowered through the roof. In the midst of his own sermon, and moved by his own intentions, the fully human Jesus must have—at least for a moment—experienced the anxiety and inside churning that come to all of us when interrupted in the work we are about.

And finally, I think they achieve what they are about, both in the book and in the faith empowerment process described, through compassion. Throughout the text, there is an awe and a reverence toward the people in this process, and toward the joys and the hopes, the pain and the despair in their lives. There is a feeling-for, a suffering-with, and a sabbatical capacity to wait manifested here. And if we are willing to join them in this activity, as well as the broader activities described so beautifully here, we shall undoubtedly become better able to embody a similar compassion ourselves. And—amazing grace—we shall have learned that our own understandings of scripture, of imagination and of faith are richer because of reading this book than when we first believed.

MARIA HARRIS
New York City

Scripture and Imagination

1/Tales to Tell

I remember well the night when we were all listening to Barbara. Barbara is a deeply caring, sensitive woman of fifty, perpetually young in spirit. Some months before, while she and her daughter were accompanying her husband on a business trip to New York City, she was mugged. Barbara chose to relive this event as her faith empowering group "presentation." She had been walking along with her husband and daughter when she was pounced upon from the side. Her almost unseen attacker lunged for the gold chain around her neck. He did manage to break it from her and race away, casting her into the gutter. She remembers lying down over a sewer grate, face down into the debris. On top of the trash glistened the flower that had been on the chain. Later on, she would affirm that flower's survival as a sign for her of hope and promise.

As she lived through the episode again, we felt many of her feelings, and were touched and moved by her response. How typical of Barbara to find the "flower" in the midst of pain and hurt—and garbage!

But there was, of course, far more to the session than this story. After empathizing with Barbara, the leader turned us to a pre-selected scripture passage, the story of the Gerasene demoniac (or person who is mentally deranged):

> "They came to the other side of the sea, to the country of the Gerasenes. And when he [Jesus] had come out of the boat, there met him out of the tombs a man with an unclean spirit, who lived among the tombs; and no one could bind him any more, even with a chain; for he had often been bound with fetters and chains, but the chains he wrenched apart, and the fetters he broke in pieces; and no one had the strength to subdue him." (Mark 5:1-4)

1

After the leader read a guided meditation composed for that evening session, our group's free-associations flowed forth, as we tried to make imaginative connections between Barbara's life experience and the particular biblical story we had just heard. There was the obvious comparison of the violent contemporary attacker with the violent ancient demoniac. There was the strangeness of New York for Barbara as a New Englander, a strangeness which made that huge and alien city feel much like "the other side of the sea" in the biblical story.

But we went far, far beyond that. We risked a playful comparison of Barbara herself with the demoniac, given her wild, flaying, uncontrolled feelings of fear and panic in the moments of the attack. We felt the need to personalize the attacker and to understand his needs. Ironically, Barbara is the kind of person who would gladly have given him the gold chain, had he but asked. And there was the interplay in the group discussion between the chains about the Gerasene and the gold chain around Barbara's neck. How is such a modern chain of gold also a fetter?

Barbara then shared that she had heard on the radio that very day a need for volunteer helpers at a shelter for battered women. She was beginning to feel a new benefit coming out of this pain, a flower to be retrieved from the trash. She was reaching for new empathy for the victims of assault or of violence of any type. She saw a way, finally, that God might be calling her out of this trauma into ministry to others.

*   *   *

For over six years as many as five groups of eight to twelve persons have come together monthly to seek a more powerful faith. They have brought with them their personal stories, their faith journeys, their riskings, trustings and grapplings with each other and with God. What we would like to do in this first chapter is to share portions from several faith empowering sessions—such as the one above—to enable you to get a sense of what can happen in such groups. These stories are the flesh and sinew which must be put on the skeleton of the actual process. And these stories may give you a feeling for the contribution which a faith empowering group can make in people's lives. The testimony is then but a witness to the empowering of faith through an unleashed biblical imagination.

*   *   *

On another night, one of us can still remember how the biblical images came alive. We were seated together in Margaret's darkened family room, and Don had just finished a tale of his visit to Russia with a "Bridges for Peace" delegation. He had shared the overwhelming power of a special painting of Rembrandt's Sacrifice of Isaac, located in the Hermitage in Leningrad. One association he had made immediately with the painting was a peace sermon, "Walking to Mt. Moriah," preached on that Genesis 22 text in his own church before his departure. He had been reduced to tears at this moment of both viewing and remembering. There in Russia was the same testimony to faith and sacrifice that filled the ancient scriptural story, the precarious balance between a God of love and the holocaust-like forces of destruction. The balance was there, not in missiles, but within humanity, within even Abraham, "the father of our faith."

Indeed, Don shared much more than this kernel. Our small group relaxed into our seats as he concluded his presentation, obviously seeking clues to his own calling in peace ministry. But it was time to put his story aside for just a few minutes, and to go on another excursion into the storyscape of the scripture passage chosen for this faith empowering session. Dusk had settled into dark in the room, yet Margaret did not stir to turn on lights. And so the leader began to read the "famous" passage at the beginning of Isaiah 6. How many times I had passed over those words at surface levels before. . . Ho hum . . . "In the year that King Uzziah died I saw the Lord sitting upon a throne, high and lifted up; and [God's] train filled the temple. Above [God] stood the seraphim. . . ." But this time it was different! My inner eyes were open, and I saw those bizarre six-winged seraphim, as though they were all around our gathered circle, peering down into us in the dark.

From the actual reading of Isaiah, the leader moved into a guided meditation on the biblical text. Again, all around me, I could hear the words coming through the reader as though they were spoken by the chanting seraphim: "Holy, holy, holy is the Lord of hosts; the *whole earth* is full of [God's] glory." I remember only the movements in the fantasy as I let my imagination run free:

> The room filled with smoke, the cold hearth erupted in flame, and a seraphim took tongs from the fireplace set and produced a glowing briquette. And the seraphim went about the group with the coal, and seared each person's lips, only no one cried out. When this eight-foot seraphim came my way, I braced, but his eyes had authority. He touched me and my lips tingled like novocaine. I more than heard, yet did not fully understand—although I understood far more than I ever had before.

And then the leader invited us to offer—still with our eyes closed— any images, associations, insights, feelings that came to mind or to heart from the biblical passage and guided meditation. We shared a pool of images which might help the presenter to find new insight in the discussion to follow. As so many times before in our group, the images tumbled forth gently and steadily.

Getting Started

We are now ready for an overview of the faith empowering process. Each session has two major parts, the two being separated in time: a preparation meeting in advance (see chapter nine) and the actual group meeting itself (described in detail in chapter two and elaborated in chapters three through eight). No moment of insight and power can be programmed, to be sure, but it is possible to devise processes which are conducive to growth in faith, or at least to moments of illumination.

How is a faith empowering session "organized?" A faith empowering group is normally composed of eight to twelve people who may or may not have any training in the Bible. Typically groups meet monthly over the course of a year. Quite simply, for each session two persons in the group, the *leader* who is to *lead* that particular group session, and the *presenter* who is to *share a piece of personal experience,* meet in a preparation session with an advisor to the process. The latter must be an individual of personal sensitivity and some biblical knowledge. In that advance time together, the presenter shares his or her thoughts for the meeting to come. All three persons discuss and clarify how best to utilize the steps in the process for this particular presentation. Then all three search for an appropriate scripture passage. The scripture is best chosen intuitively. How this is done is well described for now by the following reconstruction from an actual preparation session.

*   *   *

Paul, Jeanne, and I met for breakfast one morning, and as soon as we had our coffee, Paul, the presenter, started to talk. He is a hospital administrator who had started routinely some time ago to visit a woman long confined to the intensive care unit. Previously the woman had been an acquaintance of his, but the relationship now deepened into one of pastoral care.

Paul felt that a natural next step in the progression of the relationship was to pray with her, but he felt awkward doing so. Who was he as an administrator (and a lay person) to step into the role of chaplain in such a busy and visible place as the intensive care unit? Staff members might question the appropriateness of his behavior. And there was his own inner block, as much as he felt compelled in that direction.

We sat back in our chairs as Paul finished, taking a few pokes at breakfast. After we had engaged Paul in a bit more conversation about this relationship, I asked if a scripture passage occurred to either of them which might "work" for this presentation. Paul shook his head, and my mind was a blank. A funny, amused look came across Jeanne's face and lit up her ever-sparkling eyes. "I don't know why I've thought of this," she said, "because it makes absolutely no sense to me, but I've got one thought."

"Trust it," I encouraged her. "What is it?"

"Well, for some reason the story of Jesus with the woman caught in the act of adultery comes to mind; the passage where the men wanted to stone her." (The story is in John 7:53—8:11, a passage which is not included in the main body of the text of the Revised Standard Version, but is included in a footnote at the bottom of that page in the Bible.) We all laughed, because it did indeed make no sense—at first. In the moment of laughter, however, my mind "computed" the perfect imaginative fit of this passage. How similar were some of the dynamics! In the one instance, a modern woman is caught in the extremity of her hospital bed, her privacy and dignity constantly "violated" by the multitudes of caregivers. And in the other instance, an ancient woman is cast in total vulnerability as well, before an angry crowd. Paul was also feeling some of the awkwardness, the "nakedness," of his own exposure, wanting some of the spiritual authority of Jesus within the crowded ward but wondering how he could claim that authority in a role-conscious modern hospital without the actual role or garb of chaplain. The interplay could go in many other directions. The scriptural choice was fortuitous.

Of course, the choice does not often come so perfectly or readily, and we have often "sweat bullets" while scanning scripture aggressively as we tried to find a suitable choice. Yet, all of us, every time we use this process, are becoming more and more biblically literate, and are finding the relevance of scripture for life in fresh new ways.

It is time to invite you into the process in a fuller way, by sharing the whole story of an actual faith empowering session from beginning to end—one in which one of the authors was the presenter, and as it happened, the other the leader. . . .

An Actual Session

The warm crackling of the fire on a bleak fall morning welcomed our group as we joined together, greeting each other and settling down with our coffee cups. Bill led us in a very brief opening sharing and prayer, in which he asked for God's presence to be with me (Joe) as I shared my story.

I had decided to reflect with the group upon two episodes in my life, involving the three key women in my life: the death of my mother and the birth of my daughter. As I had searched for something to share with our group, I had realized how important it was for me to share the hours I spent with my mother as she drew her last breaths, and as she finally submitted to her battle with emphysema. Likewise, I needed to share another hospital vigil of mine a year later involving the birth of my daughter and Caesarean surgery upon my wife. I needed to discern the pulse of God in these pulsings of life and death to ventilate these moments which touched me so deeply.

And so I spun out the particulars of my mother's last days. I shared with the group how I settled into the bedside chair, on what I sensed to be her last night, to see her through this death-birthing, for which a life of tenacious faith had well prepared her. The mood in the room was not unlike the muted expectancy of Christmas Eve. All that can be done had been. It was a waiting time. . . . I rose from the chair near dawn as I sensed a change and knew that her deteriorating lungs were struggling for their last breaths. Instinctively, I found myself sitting on the edge of her bed, like an orchestra leader, gently "conducting" with circular motions those breaths of her spirit up and out of her body. I wanted somehow to lift her spirit up as she shucked her battered shell. I shed quiet tears as I beheld the irrevocable moment. And the death frost of winter settled in. For a long time I sat there, not moving. . . .

My pause permitted some sighs from group members who caught the feeling of this experience. I shifted to another episode, which stood in continuity and contrast. Certainly, no such peace or privacy prevailed at the birth of my daughter! Seven persons were gathered in the operating room for this Caesarean delivery. My attention was almost all fixed upon my wife's eyes, draped from the action as we were, until I was invited to rise for the moment of birth. Our newborn was lifted up into the blinding light, a startled scowl upon her face, her body turning rosy even as her spirit purpled! The wail allayed our deepest fears; the revelation of her gender fulfilled the hope we dared not express too much. I was conscious even then of how reverse this was to the process of death I had previously witnessed—now purple to pink, then pink to purple. And then somewhat regrettably perhaps, my eyes focused upon the seemingly mortal wound across my wife's abdomen. I could see, too, the bright red hues of her insides, a sight from which I later wished I had been spared! I was overwhelmed with how vulnerable and destructible life is; how expendably, yet how inexorably, the life process itself flows from generation to generation. . . . Soon my hands were full, as the nurse diverted me to wiping off and holding this daughter of mine.

I stopped there, with more feeling inside me than I had realized. Group members reflected back some of those feelings, just enough to let me know they had really heard me and were ready and willing to be present with me as we proceeded. Then I relaxed into the next step of the process, the scripture passage and guided meditation from the story of David and Absalom in 2 Samuel.

"Sit comfortably," Bill's voice directed. "Close your eyes and focus for a moment on your breathing. . . . As you inhale, feel the renewing presence of the Spirit flowing through your body. . . . As you exhale, let the pressures and tensions which face you this day drain away. . . . Listen with the ear of your imagination. . . .

"You are David—rich, handsome, strong, popular. Life, for the most part, has come your way. You took on Goliath—and you won. You desired Bathsheba— and you took her. (Yes, God was angry with you for Bathsheba, and when you realized what you had done, you broke down and wept. But you still kept Bathsheba.) You are the king—you have a kingdom, you have children, you have power. . . .

"Absalom is your son. He, too, is rich, handsome, and strong. Yet he is not as popular as you are. Life has not gone as well for him as it has for you—or maybe it is that life has come too easily for him—or maybe he has always had to live life in your shadow. Absalom, for one, has never learned how to weep, the way you can. He has learned how to be jealous, however. . . . And now he is stirring up the people, mobilizing all their restlessness, their frustration, their unmet needs. Absalom is leading a rebellion against you—his father. . . .

"Picture Absalom in your mind. What do you see? . . . How do you feel toward him? . . . Do you want him to succeed in his rebellion? . . . Do you want him to fail? . . . What do you want for Absalom? . . .

"Now the battle is joined between your soldiers and the soldiers of Absalom. You, yourself, are not fighting, but you can hear the noises of war in the distance. Minutes become hours—and still no word. How are you feeling as you wait? . . .

"The noise dies down. The dust cloud on the horizon begins to settle. In the distance, you see a scout, running toward you. You strain to make out the expression on his face. What are you hoping to hear? . . .

"The scout comes running up to you, and, breathing hard, blurts out that there is good news: You have won again! How does winning make you feel? . . .

"You cannot wait—you ask how it is with the young man, Absalom. And the scout, loyal to the end, cries out proudly: 'May everyone who rises against you meet the same fate as he met today!' (adapted from 2 Samuel 18:32)

"Slowly, the meaning of the words sinks in. Absalom is dead. Absalom, your son, is dead. Your mind is filled with flashbacks: Absalom's birth from his mother's womb into your waiting arms . . . . Absalom, the boy, trying to imitate your every move. . . . Absalom, the adolescent, stormily lashing out at you . . . leaving you paralyzed in your ability to communicate with him. . . . You remember the deep hurt you felt when you heard he was stirring up a rebellion against you—the fear, the anger, the competitiveness. . . . But he is still your son. And you are still his father. And he is dead. Something inside you has died, too. Feel the grief within you. Let it come, flowing as it will. . . . Feel the memories it brings with it. . . . Feel the fears it pushes ahead of it. . . .

"O my son Absalom, my son, my son Absalom! Would I had died instead of you, O Absalom, my son, my son!" . . . (verse 33b)

There was a long pause. Then the leader finished the meditation by saying to the group:

"As you are ready, take some time to live into the feelings and images that come to your mind from this story. And share these, as you wish, in a word or a phrase with the group."

Gradually again the group began to share. I was glad, at first as the presenter, to remain silent during this step of the meeting, for I was both confused and primed. This meditation did not initially seem to relate much to the episodes I had shared, for its maleness tended to evoke my relationship with my own father and my own son. But the feelings had built up inside me, nonetheless. I remember the connection between my moments of waiting for death and for life and David's waiting for news, both of us unable to influence the outcome.

Then someone mentioned David's "kingly" authority, and the authority they had felt me express at my dying mother's bedside. The group went on to share images relating to the acceptance of life's flow, the course of events beyond one's control, grief and grace, power and powerlessness, authority and its limits.

The leader invited me back into the process to share actively. I think it was Val who said something about "prophet, priest, and king," John Calvin's offices of Christ and three roles for the Christian. This struck me with all the force of a clue. I felt that for many years in many ways I had prepared for the roles of prophet and priest. Indeed, one can be educated in biblical consciousness and pastoral caring. But only life can educate the "king." Here was an unexpected insight, a suggestively rich range, yet with humbling limitations.

I was immediately brought back to my collegiate fascination with tragic heroes—with Lear, with Job, and other foolhardy seekers. I talked with the group about a style of authority which is personal, familial, and professional—able to influence, but not to control. We spoke of David and Christ as models, and the limitations of male perspectives on power. We were bringing in topics I had long neglected in my life of fate, character, and destiny: life-forces that take me beyond my pastoral skills and prophetic voice into my own participation in life's movement beyond my control. The episodes I had shared felt freshly connected to all of my life; I felt moved from mastery into mystery. David sobbed for me, and my life flowed anew on his river of tears.

We shared an implication of our time together for our own faith. And we closed our time together with prayer. I still sat, feeling graced by a God who could be accepting both of my power and powerlessness within the transforming events of life and death in my own life story.

* * *

Certainly, this is only the gist of our time together. The group session did not go where I had expected, but serendipitously, I felt much more connected and grounded in a sense of personal destiny, and in God's presence in tragic, comic, and everyday events of my life. I had gained fresh personal insight into interests which had formerly been largely intellectual, for I had never connected the theme of personal authority with the role of the "kingly" in me.

But there are other tales to tell! Now it is time to tell the story of this process itself, which audaciously seeks to empower faith!

2/*Summarizing the Steps*

"Faith is a search for meaning, a covenant in shared exploration." (A faith empowering group member's comment, on April 25, 1982.)

"I was born lame. I have been carried to this place for as long as I can remember. It is a good place to beg—this entrance to the temple. It has allowed me, at least, to eat and keep myself in necessary clothing.

"It is, however, a very long day. I must wait until three o'clock when the hour of prayer begins and the traffic increases, and also the alms.

"I sit here now watching the people pass me by. Time hangs over me like a shroud—waiting to cover me completely. Not them. Time—I have so much of it. People going by. Always going by. Running, walking, hurrying by. They barely notice me—crouched, misshaped, leaning against the temple wall. I watch their faces—empty faces, frustrated faces, faceless faces. They are always in a hurry. Their faces show the anxiety of the time. They are depressed. They are stern. They lack emotion. Only the children smile.

"Mornings and evenings. More people pass by then. Rushing to work, to school, to appointments.

"But it will be three o'clock soon. And the day will be brighter for me. I wonder what it would be like to walk. To run. . . ."

This was how a lay person started a guided meditation based on the story of Peter and John and the man lame from birth, at the Beautiful Gate of the temple in Jerusalem. This is the story where Peter says, "I have no silver and gold, but I give you what I have; in the name of Jesus Christ of Nazareth, walk." (Acts 3:1–10; especially verse 6)

"I was born lame. . . ." Immediately we identify; we try to imagine ourselves as the beggar. . . .

What are these guided meditations all about? They are a part of the six-step faith empowering process. They are an attempt in the third step to enable a small group to enter imaginatively into the meanings of a biblical passage. A guided meditation, then, is a way to prime the pump of group imagination, a pump from which we believe flows the living water of a growing spirituality.

Guided meditations in the faith empowering process are an attempt to enable a group of people to participate imaginatively in biblical material, such as the Acts passage above. But, as we at least, have been using such meditations, they are also an attempt to enable that same group of people to enter imaginatively into a portion of the contemporary life experience of one of its members. Indeed, the guided meditation might be defined as a **bridge** between a slice of life experience today and a slice of biblical experience—a bridge on which human imagination is free to roam and play and dance.

The other critical building-block step of the faith empowering process, step two of our six-step model, revolves around a **personal presentation,** in which a member of the group shares a piece of his or her personal experience that one would like to have reflected on in the context both of faith and of a supportive group. When it is your turn to be presenter, you can choose what you want to share—and what you do not want to share—in your personal presentation. Usually it is enough to say to a future presenter, who is wondering what to present, something like the following: "Choose some part of your life where faith, broadly understood, is a growing edge." Over the years of our experience with the six-step process, we have come to trust that presenters are able to name their own issues or concerns.

In the case of the faith empowering session described at the beginning of this chapter, the presenter had shared his own concern about the issue of **time**—how he felt there was never enough of it to go around to all the many facets of his life, each of them important. The woman who led that session picked up this theme when she wrote in her guided meditation:

"I sit here now watching the people pass me by. Time hangs over me like a shroud—waiting to cover me completely. Not them. Time—I have so much of it. People going by. Always going by. Running, walking, hurrying by. They barely notice me—crouched, misshaped, leaning against the temple wall. I watch their faces—empty faces, frustrated faces, faceless faces. They are always in a hurry. Their faces show the anxiety of the time. They are depressed. They are stern. They lack emotion. Only the children smile."

But the deeper beauty of this particular guided meditation is also found in the bridge it makes with the image of lameness. The story in Acts is about a man "lame from birth." And the mood of the presenter's sharing of contemporary experience was of the disabling effect that crowded, hurried time had on his own sense of meaning in life. If "faith is a search for meaning, a covenant in shared exploration," as the quote at the beginning of this chapter describes it, then the presenter's sharing was a faith issue: a search for healing from the laming, paralyzing effects of time's passing. Through the guided meditation, the faith empowering group was enabled to forge imaginative connections between the lame man two thousand years ago at the Beautiful Gate, and the presenter of today who never seemed to have enough time. And that presenter was free to draw from the connections made by the group for his own growth and deepening in faith.

We have described the heart of the faith empowering process, the imaginative bridge between a presentation from contemporary personal experience and scripture. Around that heart there is much more: preparation sessions, the role of an enabler, selecting the best scripture passage for a particular faith empowering session, the role of scripture in a session, the role imagination plays, etc. We would also like to share the relationship of faith empowering to the emerging field of faith development. And we would like to offer enough illustrative material to give life and depth to discussions of process. But let us begin with a summary description of the six-step faith empowering process.

Faith Empowering Process—A Summary

STEP 1/SHARING AND PRAYER
The leader of the particular faith empowering group session will ask members of the group to share in a brief "community building" exercise related to the theme that the meeting will be considering, and the leader will then offer a prayer.

STEP 2/PERSONAL HORIZON
The presenter for that session shares a piece of personal experience in a way that is comfortable. The leader guides the rest of the group to respond with active listening.

STEP 3/BIBLICAL HORIZON
The leader reads a pre-selected passage from scripture. The leader helps the

group to live imaginatively into the the biblical passage and the personal presentation from step two through a pre-written guided meditation.

STEP 4/POOLING IMAGES

During this step, the presenter listens quietly. The leader invites the rest of the group—still in the mood of relaxed meditation—to share as many images and feelings as possible that come to mind from the biblical passage and guided meditation of step three, and from the personal presentation of step two.

STEP 5/MAKING CONNECTIONS—MERGING HORIZONS

The leader invites the group to come out of its meditative state, and the presenter to rejoin the conversation. The leader then helps the presenter and the rest of the group to work in partnership to focus the points of connection between the presenter's personal presentation, the Bible passage, and the guided meditation, and to probe the meaning of those connections.

STEP 6/CLOSING SHARING AND PRAYER

The leader invites each group member, including the presenter, to share whatever personal implications or directions for the future the session may have brought to light. The leader then offers the experience of that faith empowering group meeting to God in prayer.

SUPPLEMENTARY INFORMATION

PREPARATION SESSION

Each faith empowering group needs an enabler who will meet in advance of every faith empowering session for that group with the presenter and leader for that session. These preparation sessions are intended to hear and focus the presenter's sharing, to select a relevant biblical passage for that sharing, and to review the leadership needs and possibilities for the session's leader.

SUGGESTED TIMING

Each group meeting will want to work out its own sense of timing for the six steps above. One suggested timing is as follows: step one—10 minutes; step two—20 minutes; step three—20 minutes; step four—15 minutes; step five—20 minutes; step six—20 minutes. The total session would then last about one hour and 45 minutes.

The chapters that follow will offer a more detailed elaboration of each of the six steps of the faith empowering process, along with background and illustrative material as appropriate.

3/Sharing and Prayer

STEP 1: SHARING AND PRAYER. The leader for the particular faith empowering group session will convene the meeting. That leader will ask members of the group to share in a brief "community building" exercise (such as giving each person the opportunity to respond to a simple question) around the theme that the meeting will be considering. The leader concludes this step of the process with a prayer, reflecting, if possible, the sharing which the group has just done, and asking for God's presence to be especially with the presenter for the session.

Much has been written on the importance of "community building" for group meetings. These writings affirm the value of building a spirit of community among all the members of a group by actively reaching out at the beginning of a meeting to invite each person to participate. Certainly, names need to be shared in groups of people where not everybody knows everybody else. But that is not enough. Community building must go deeper than that.

Groups can create a deep spirit of community if there is an opportunity to share feelings. Some people, for perfectly valid reasons, may choose not to share out loud at a given session, and the freedom to pass must be respected if the group is to build a climate of non-coercive trust. But most of us, most of the time, are willing to respond to carefully chosen community building questions or exercises—and we feel a sense of inclusion in the group as we do.

You are obviously free, and encouraged, to use your own creativity in developing community building ideas. But you are also free to borrow—as we have—good ideas from other people. Some sample community building suggestions we have used include the following:

Sample Community Building Suggestions

1/Give an adjective which best describes the day you have had today.

2/If you had to paint a picture of your last week, what would be the major color you would use?

3/If your life at present could be imaged in a musical instrument, what instrument would that be for you?

4/If you could be a plant or flower in a garden, what would you choose to be—and why?

5/Describe your life right now by naming a body of water that symbolizes it (running stream, clear pool, raging sea, etc.).

6/Pass around some play-dough and ask people to mold it in shapes which express a particular feeling, and then share and discuss the shape and their feelings.

In a faith empowering group session, it is particularly helpful if the community building question or exercise relates in a general way to the theme, issue, or concern that the presenter will be sharing in step two. (That being the case, we have encouraged the presenter to pass in step one, since he or she will have ample opportunity to share in a moment.) When the question of step one relates to the theme of step two, the imagination of the group is already focused and enlisted for its later work of image-pooling. And the presenter, who on occasion may be taking a risk by the intended sharing of step two, is usually reassured by the group's comments in step one: the presenter can come to feel in an important way that he or she is not alone in the concern of the presentation and that the risk of sharing is both possible and valuable. The community building exercise, then, can serve the important function of giving the group's "permission" and encouragement to the presenter to share the depth of a particular piece of personal experience.

There are practical factors that come into play in the choice of a community building idea. An obvious example is the length of time it will take. The goal of the faith empowering group session is to focus on the empowerment of the presenter's faith. That goal would be undermined if the rest of the group shared at such length and detail in step one that there was neither time nor energy left to deal with steps two through six! The leader of the session needs to help the group to discipline itself to share in enough depth to "prepare the ground" for the presenter, but not to overwhelm the process with a flood of step one sharing that leaves the presenter on the periphery of the session.

We have found it generally helpful to use a few minutes of the *preparation session* to plan the community building for the coming faith empowering session. It is best to deal with community building ideas towards the end of the preparation session, after the theme of the presenter's sharing, and the relevant biblical passage, have been determined. Such planning can assist the leader, reassure the presenter, and make the group meeting that much more valuable for all concerned.

We will list below a few more examples of community building ideas, this time listing along with those ideas the general theme of step two, in order to illustrate the relationship between the community building of step one and the personal presentation of step two:

Community Building and
Personal Presentation Themes

SOME EXAMPLES

GENERAL THEME	COMMUNITY BUILDER
1/Concern about values and money.	Pass around a well-worn dollar bill and share your feelings about it.
2/The presenter's experience of being a minister (the ministry of the laity).	Describe where you are in your own ministry through images from a track meet. (Some responses when this was used: entering the decathlon, serving as a hurdle, injured in the Red Cross tent, organizing the meet, discovering one's name somehow scratched from the event but entering it anyway.)
3/Relationship with one's father.	Describe the favorite activity you remember doing with your father (or with a father figure).
4/Coming to terms with a broken relationship.	The presenter, when this was used, was an artist. He had painted a simple picture of the most recent experience of that broken relationship, and group members were asked to pass the uninterpreted painting around the circle and share the feelings it evoked.

| 5/**Coming to terms with fear.** | Read the opening to Dr. Seuss' story about pale green pants, "What Was I Scared Of?"[1] and ask each group member to share what pale green pants might represent in their own life. |

Step one concludes with prayer. And this is important. The community we are seeking to build is not only the fellowship of other persons, but also the fellowship of the Holy Spirit. The one is rooted in the other. Neither fellowship can simply be created on demand, but if faith is to be empowered, we need to honor both the human beings who are with us in our searching and the divine Spirit whose underlying presence is the foundation of all that we do.

Not every participant in a faith empowering group is comfortable with the experience of leading a group in public prayer. One person, who has proved quite adept at every other part of the six-step process, has commented that, for the group leader, this prayer-leadership responsibility in step one (and again in step six) may be the scariest part of faith empowering! Obviously, there is room in a total faith empowering program for retreats or workshops on prayer and spirituality.

Some faith empowering group leaders have found it helpful to write out all or part of the prayer in advance (either composing it themselves or using a prayer written by someone else). We have found it valuable to encourage leaders to leave at least a part of their step one prayer open to spontaneity. When such openness is allowed, leaders can take notes of a key word or phrase from the community building sharing of each group member, and then lift that word or phrase up to God, as a way of deepening the spirit of the group.

An example may be helpful here of the way in which such a prayer can incorporate the community building sharing. Suppose the community building question were: Describe your life right now by naming a body of water that symbolizes it? A prayer might pick up on the community building sharing as follows: "Dear God, we come to you as several people seeking to let our energies flow around Bob tonight. We come feeling like little puddles, mountain streams in springtime, thunderous deeps, bottled-up office water-cooler jars, mudflats at low tide, or clear lakes sparkling in the sunlight. May whatever comes of this time together be of value for us all. In Jesus' name we pray. Amen."

A crucial part of the step one prayer is a request for God's presence to be with the presenter. We have already mentioned the sense of risk that presenters often feel in sharing a piece of personal experience. The experience of being held in prayer by name can help the presenter to take the risk. And the prayer for God's presence can be a helpful reminder to everyone that it is God who is the ultimate source of whatever empowering of faith there may be.

4/Presenting Our Stories

STEP 2: PERSONAL HORIZON. The presenter for that session shares a piece of personal experience in a way that is comfortable; the presenter shares from within his or her own "horizon of meaning" and is encouraged to share in as personal a way as possible. The leader guides the rest of the group to respond with active listening—to understand and empathize, reflecting back what people have heard and felt from the presenter, without trying to solve or judge anything or anyone.

To begin with, what do we mean by the term "horizon?" We will use that term in this chapter in relation to "personal horizon" and "horizon of meaning." Later on, during our discussion of step three in chapter five, we will be talking about the "biblical horizon" of a passage. What do we mean by the term "horizon" in that context as well?

The term is both a technical word in the field of biblical interpretation and an everyday word. And the technical and everyday meanings are related. Let us begin, briefly, with a technical definition. The German philosopher, Hans-Georg Gadamer, writes, "The horizon is the range of vision that includes everything that can be seen from a particular vantage point."[1] Horizons are not fixed boundaries. "The horizon is, rather, something into which we move and that moves with us. Horizons change for a person who is moving."[2]

What is Gadamer saying? We may start from the everyday, common sense meaning of horizon. Take a minute, if you will, stop reading, and look up all around you. You will see a horizon. If you are inside a building, your horizon will be bounded for the most part with walls and pictures, ceiling and floor, furniture and any other people or objects in the room. Where there are windows, your horizon will extend to the out-of-doors, with its buildings, sky, trees, streets, snow, flowers.

When a faith empowering group presenter shares a piece of personal experience, part of the "horizon of meaning" is the simple physical horizon visible around him or her. In fact, getting in touch with that visible horizon is a way of getting in touch with profound feelings about our personal experience within that horizon. Think for a moment about the feelings associated with the visible horizon from a hospital bed, or the kitchen in your childhood home, or the top of a mountain on a crystal clear day in fall foliage season, or an empty house at three o'clock in the morning!

When we move from a visible horizon to the feelings evoked by that horizon, we are beginning to move from the everyday, common sense meaning of the word to its more technical sense, as well as its more imaginative and expanded sense. Return, if you will, to your own particular horizon at this moment. Beyond the physically visible horizon, there are other elements of an expanded sense of horizon. There are personal elements that affect what you "see" and which are, hence, a part of your horizon: your health, your age, your employment situation, the present tone or mood of important relationships, past or future-projected crises, etc. There are general historical elements that are a part of our horizon: the state of the economy, the changing roles of men and women, world tensions. There are scientific-technological elements in our horizon: we understand today that the earth revolves around the sun, that germs can cause disease, that we can travel across the United States in a few hours, that human life is conceived when a sperm enters and fertilizes an egg, that a nuclear holocaust is all too possible.

Our personal horizon can be enormously affected by our race, sex, age, class, religion. The horizon may include not just what we see, but what we hear and smell and taste and feel. What we have experienced from the inside will fill our horizon in a different way from what we have only read about or heard about from others.

Obviously, not all of the elements that make up the horizon of a particular experience are equally relevant in shaping the way we give meaning to that experience. When a presenter shares a piece of personal experience in step two of the faith empowering process, he or she must do some prioritizing. The point is, however, that the meaning we give to an experience is related to the horizon within which we receive that experience. Articulating the horizon of a life event is a way of getting at the meaning we are giving to it. And, if as we quoted at the beginning of chapter two: "Faith is a search for meaning, a covenant in shared exploration," articulating the horizon of a life event is a way of getting at its faith dimension.

One other point about horizons: one way to change the meaning of a life event is to change the horizon of that event. Horizons can change in a variety of ways. Horizons can broaden or be refined or reformed through experience, for example, or by travel or education. Horizons can change as our own outlook is brought face-to-face with the differing horizons of other people whose ideas and feelings we care about or need to hear. Horizons change imperceptibly but inevitably as we ourselves grow and develop through life's different ages or stages.

Fundamentally, faith empowering is about the changing of horizons so that the faith meaning of an event can be transformed. The horizon of meaning of a presenter is brought face-to-face with the horizon of meaning of scripture in the context of the supportive, imaginative probing of horizons by a faith empowering group. The goal is that the presenter will find new insight and a new accompanying release of energy along with that insight. No process can guarantee fulfillment of such a goal, but we are encouraged by our experience to affirm the goal as a realistic hope. It can happen!

We have said that presenters are challenged to choose for presentation some part of their life where faith, broadly understood, is a growing edge. And we have affirmed that such a challenge is usually sufficient to call forth the kind of presentations that can lead to a meaningful faith empowering experience. There is more, however, which can be said about personal presentations in this process. We have, in fact, gathered a number of useful guidelines:

Guidelines for Personal Presentations

FAITH EMPOWERING GROUPS

1/No areas of life concern should be ruled out automatically, as faith pertains to all of life.

2/Some areas of life concern might be set aside, or postponed to a later faith empowering session, for perfectly valid reasons—there may be too much material for the presenter to cover in one session; the material may be too sensitive at this time for the presenter to hope to gain from sharing it; the material may not be appropriate to share in the presence of one or more of the other members of the faith empowering group; etc.

3/If there is a question about the appropriateness of a particular personal presentation, that question should be discussed in the preparation session.

4/The idea of a personal presentation should not necessarily be equated with a *problem;* and the purpose of a faith empowering session is not to be seen as trying to find an *answer* or a *solution.* Personal presentations are best seen as the *sharing of issues or concerns.*

5/Presentations need not always be based on life's heaviest or darkest moments or concerns. Joys may be profitably shared to celebrate their deeper meanings.

6/Imagination is encouraged in every step of the faith empowering process, including step two. Topics may be based on the past or the present, but they might also involve an imaginative living-in to the future.

7/Presentations based on intellectual or abstract belief issues are most helpfully explored in the faith empowering process when these can be personalized and linked to life experience.

8/The presenter has a fundamental responsibility for the selection of material to be presented, and the extent of its elaboration. Leaders need to be sensitive to boundaries which the presenter may wish to impose.

9/We strongly emphasize that *there is no expectation that the presenter will bare his soul or spill her guts.* Our own experience with faith empowering groups to date has shown a great human sensitivity to the one who is risking the personal sharing in step two, allowing that person to share only what he or she wants to share.

The actual topics that people have covered in faith empowering groups are widely varied. One group spent its first year with each person sharing his or her own "master story" or "life story" in brief. No one in that group intended at the outset the presenting of "master stories," but the sharing which evolved was, nonetheless, enormously valuable for the whole group. That group then went on in subsequent years to focus more on single episodes or events from individual presenter's lives.

In general (though with important deviations from the pattern) groups have focused more on issues of *identity*—"Who am I?"—in their early group life, and then turned gradually to issues of *ministry*—"What am I doing, and what does what I'm doing or not doing have to do with my faith?"—as the groups have continued.

A few of the actual themes of faith empowering presentations include:

• aloneness
• relationship with a relative

- coping with a mother's dying
- living faithfully in an affluent suburb
- the tension between Christian faith and materialism
- coping with the anxiety of illness
- how to keep social compassion alive in today's world
- how to accept God's love
- how to find a more personal relationship with Jesus
- letting go and trusting
- what to do about guilt when it is immobilizing
- coping with pressures of business decisions
- coping with depression as a staff person in a hospital for the chronically ill

Many more examples could be given, but the above list suggests the range of possibilities.

After the presenter has shared his or her piece of personal experience, the faith empowering group responds with "active listening." By such active listening we mean an attempt by the group to reflect back to the presenter what people have heard, and particularly what people are feeling, from the presenter. The point of such active listening is not to judge or try to answer the presentation, but rather to give the presenter the opportunity to know that she has been heard or to clarify places where he has not been heard. The non-judgmental, supportive mirroring in active listening is an important way to embrace the presenter who has just risked the sharing of personal experience. As the presenter feels both held and heard, he or she can be encouraged to open his or her horizon of meaning to change and growth.

Sometimes, faith empowering groups want to respond to the personal presentation of step two by asking the presenter questions of clarification or elaboration. Whereas some question-asking at this point may be both inevitable and helpful, there are problems with these questions: the presenter may be pushed by an unsuspecting questioner into areas he or she would prefer not to share; and the questions may not convey to the presenter the important reassurance that he or she has been heard by the group. We would encourage groups to respond to the presenter with "I-statements" rather than questions: "What I heard you saying was . . ." or "What I feel in your presentation is . . ." or some such comment as that. By giving "I-statements," group members are risking something of themselves; and the shared sense of risk between presenter and group can be empowering for all. The presenter, of course, can respond to the "I-statements" in a number of ways: "Yes, you heard me clearly," or "No, that isn't what I meant, but let me try again," or "I hadn't thought of it that way, but you may be right."

An important dimension of step two is a gradual attempt to begin to search out the faith-focus or the faith-meaning of the presenter's sharing. Sometimes the presenter may be clear about the faith-meaning for which he or she is searching. But there will also be times when the presenter may be less clear at this point. In either case, the group may begin to search out the faith-focus during the active listening part of step two. An "I-statement" such as the following one may be helpful here: "What I hear you struggling for in terms of your faith is . . ."

The leader has no need to let the active listening continue at great length. What is important is to confirm that the group is generally aware of what the presenter is trying to say. And the group needs to begin to enter the world of imaginative reflection on the presenter's sharing. But the faith empowering process requires more input—input from scripture—before group imagination and discussion can be turned loose fully. It is time, then, for us to move on to consider step three.

5/Exploring God's Word

STEP 3: BIBLICAL HORIZON. The leader reads the pre-selected passage from scripture. The leader helps the group to live imaginatively into the biblical horizon of that passage—and the personal horizon from step two—through a pre-written guided meditation. Following the meditation, the group is invited to live into the scripture passage and guided meditation through a period of silence.

There is an intentional jump from step two of the faith empowering process to step three. During the second step the group is deeply immersed in listening to a presenter share a piece of contemporary personal experience. Then, the leader will ask the group to stop its active listening, shift gears, and listen while the leader reads a passage from the Bible. The discontinuity is both real and deliberate. And the rationale for that discontinuity is to be found in the nature of human imagination, which we turn to now.

Many of us can probably remember a time when we were struggling with a conflict of some sort, and we set that conflict aside for a while—only to discover that when we returned to it a resolution had somehow come to us. Such a relatively common phenomenon is related to the fact that our imagination keeps working even when—perhaps especially when—we take our conscious attention away from the focus of our concern.

A number of authors have written about this phenomenon. Sharon Parks, of Harvard Divinity School, uses the common word, *pause*, to describe the period of time during which we set aside a conscious conflict and await, hopefully, a flash of new insight, with its accompanying release of new energy.[1] George Prince, an expert on creativity for business and industry, speaks of the period of "incubation" which can occur when we set a problem aside and take a "vacation" from conscious attention to it.[2] Episcopal priest, Urban Holmes, wrote of the need for us to use "a certain oblique seeing" in order to discover the significant images which can describe our experience.[3] And an earlier scholar of imagination, Harold Rugg, uses the phrase, the "off-conscious,"[4] to describe the state of the human mind in which a flash of insight is generated.

The discontinuity in the six-step faith empowering process between steps two and three is related to these ideas about human imagination. The faith empowering group—and particularly the presenter—are asked to *pause* from consideration of the presenter's personal experience in order to make way for hoped-for flashes of new insight. The presentation of step two passes into a time of *incubation* as the group changes the focus of its attention over to scripture. The personal presentation does not disappear; nor does it cease its work of creative ferment. As the faith empowering group listens to a biblical passage and a guided meditation, the presenter's sharing remains in the *off-conscious* of group members, the object for each of them of a *certain oblique seeing.*

When we first began using the faith empowering process in the fall of 1980, several participants complained of a felt "choppiness" in the process, particularly between the second and third steps. After more experience, people began to feel and appreciate the built-in rhythm of the six steps. We have likened the process to a dance, whose steps may seem wooden and strange at first, but whose same steps become graceful in time.

Step three, then, involves the reading of a passage from scripture. We have already stated above that this passage is selected during the preparation session before the faith empowering group meeting (or in between the preparation session and faith empowering session, if no passage comes to mind immediately).

One way to describe how to choose the best scripture passage for a particular personal presentation is to begin by trying to identify the major emotional dynamics of the presenter's sharing, and then to identify a biblical passage which has many of those same dynamics in it—though in scrambled fashion. We will be speaking more about our understanding of the kind of biblical interpretation involved in the faith empowering process when we deal with step five: making connections—merging horizons (chapter seven). But for now we can say that the function of scripture in the faith empowering process is *not* to serve as a simple answer to the personal presentation of step two. That presentation was not intended as a "question" or a "problem" expecting an answer or solution in the first place.

The function of scripture, rather, is to provide the occasion for the amplifying, reshaping or refining of the personal horizon of the presenter. (There is also the opportunity for the presenter's horizon to bring new depth and vitality to the horizon of scripture, as people can come to feel the concrete relationship of the Bible to contemporary life.)

The crucial goal is ". . . the amplifying, reshaping or refining of the personal horizon of the presenter." And scripture is a crucial means towards that end. The personal horizon of the presenter may be warped from psychological factors, oppressed from political, or economic or sociological factors, or distorted in general through the person's particular encounter with life. And the horizon of scripture may have its own distortions, as well. Yet the faith empowering process attempts to place the personal horizon of the presenter in liberating, healing, redeeming dialogue with the Word of God in Scripture. We believe that the Holy Spirit does its liberating, healing, redeeming work at the intersections of life experience and biblical meanings.

If the particular biblical passage for a faith empowering session is to enrich the personal presentation, the biblical passage chosen needs to have substantial points of possible connection with what the presenter is sharing. What does this mean? Each personal presentation will have a number of "key elements" in it: emotions, areas of concern, significant relationships, points of tension, etc. In looking for an appropriate biblical passage for that presentation, it is helpful to try to find one that has most of the same key elements as the presentation, though not necessarily in the same order. If the biblical passage has every single one of the key elements in the presenter's sharing, the fit will probably be so neat that it will inspire little imaginative new horizon-shaping. If, on the other hand, the biblical passage has only a small number of those key elements, the relationship between scripture and personal presentation will be so distant that the horizons may not be able to engage each other in the kind of encounter which is capable of generating new insights. The two horizons—contemporary and biblical—need to be similar enough that they can stimulate creative dialogue, yet not so similar that the dialogue between them is too obvious and brief to engender much imagination.

One of the crucial reasons for having preparation sessions before the actual faith empowering group meetng is to allow for careful, reflective selection of the appropriate scripture passage for a given personal presentation. Part of the selection is intuitive—people reaching out for a passage that "somehow feels right." But part of that selection process is also amenable to pre-stated guidelines:

Guidelines for Scripture Selection ──────

FAITH EMPOWERING GROUPS

1/The advisor or enabler would be wise to ask the presenter and the leader during the preparation session if either of them has any suggestions of appropriate scripture passages, and then to offer alternatives for consideration if and as helpful.

2/Preliminary discussion in the preparation session about possible points of connection between the personal presentation and a given biblical passage can help to focus that presentation and select the most appropriate scripture.

3/The presenter should be the one to make the final selection of the biblical passage to be used in her or his faith empowering session. But the leader and enabler play crucial roles in the cross-pollination of ideas which leads to that selection.

4/The most helpful kinds of scripture material for faith empowering sessions, particularly when a group is just starting its life together, are narrative, parable, and poetry—though no passage should be ruled out. Narrative, parable, and poetry lend themselves particularly well to imaginative elaboration in guided meditation and image pooling.

5/By varying the scripture passages used by a faith empowering group, that group's working knowledge of the Bible (or what has been called its "functional canon") is increased.

6/Printed aids—such as a copy of the scripture index from the front of a *Gospel Parallels* book,[5] can be helpful in stimulating the selection process. A concordance is also a helpful reference to consult.

7/We would encourage supplementary religious education programs, with books and other resources, to give participants more biblical background for making faith empowering scripture selections.

It may be helpful at this point in time to share with you some examples of the relationship between the theme of the personal presentation and the content of the biblical passage selected for that presentation.

Scripture Selection and Personal Presentation ─┐ Theme

SOME EXAMPLES FOR ILLUSTRATION

GENERAL THEME	SCRIPTURE SELECTED
1. Lack of self-confidence.	Peter walking on the water. Matthew 14:22–32.
2. Anxiety about death in relationship to a threat of possible cancer.	Is there no balm in Gilead? Jeremiah 8:18–22.
3. Anxiety of a youth caught between mother and father in a divided and tense household.	Jesus' prediction of Peter's denial. Matthew 26:30–35.
4. A mother's impatience at house-confinement with a small baby.	Paul and Silas in jail. Acts 16:25–34.
5. A widow's search for something meaningful to do with her life.	The boy Samuel's call. 1 Samuel 3:1–10.

Guided Meditations

"It has been our experience that guided meditations have been particularly effective when written by the faith empowering group leader, though people with special facility in writing such meditations can be asked to write them for leaders who so prefer. It is helpful for a full faith empowering program to provide training and guidelines for those wishing to develop their own guided meditations."

Under "step two: Personal Horizon" above, we quoted Hans-Georg Gadamer's description of an "horizon" as "the range of vision that includes everything that can be seen from a particular vantage point."[6] We than went on to elaborate the idea of an "horizon of meaning," which includes physical elements that we can see, hear, or feel; psychological or environmental elements from our personal life; elements from history; scientific-technological elements, etc. All of those factors go into shaping the "horizon," and hence the meaning, of the presenter's personal experience.

We can now articulate what we have already hinted at: namely that a biblical passage has an horizon, too. When Jesus gave his Sermon on the Mount, for example, some of the elements of the horizon he would share with his compatriots would include: the Palestinian countryside, a relatively poor economy, Roman occupation, a belief in a three-story universe, a belief that some diseases are caused by demon-possession, a sexist culture of male dominance, etc. There would be some elements which might be common to the Bible as a whole, and some which would be particular to a given biblical passage. Some of the elements of a biblical horizon are strange to us today; some are contrary to important elements of our contemporary horizon. Yet biblical passages still deal with many of the same life issues that we struggle with today: life and death, health, sexuality, social justice, life in relationship to God, etc.

One of the basic challenges in interpreting scripture is what to do with the differing horizons of the biblical world and contemporary life; we will be dealing with this subject more fully under our discussion of "step five: making connections—merging horizons" (chapter seven). For now we may state our belief that it is as important for the empowering of faith—at least for the empowering of Jewish or Christian faith—to enter imaginatively into a biblical horizon as it is to enter imaginatively into a contemporary personal horizon. And guided meditations, as we have been using them in faith empowering groups, are a powerful means to help people enter imaginatively into the two horizons.

The psychologist Carl Jung has spoken of two types of thinking, directed and imaginal. *Directed* thinking, analytical in nature, and occurring only on the conscious plane, is the sole kind of thought to which we are accustomed. But *imaginal* thinking as the language of the deeper self is also both real and important. The latter is not only the creative thought process of the pre-logical child, but it is the language which taps the unconscious of all of us, usually occurring only in dreams. Without entering the complex inner world of dreams—which requires a skilled guide for the unpracticed—the faith empowering process taps into our imaginal world, linking our conscious thought world with the whole of experience. And that whole of experience is more than rational.

We believe that people's imagination needs help in order to be released and empowered. George Prince, the expert on creativity in business and industry whose work we cited earlier, has written:

> that nearly all of us begin life highly creative, but soon after the start of our
> formal education . . . by age eight or nine, logical, analytical thinking has taken

over. We gradually slip into the restrictive domain of traditional thought. It is in this sense that our highly analytical training restricts our creativity: we become too logical. Our rich emotional and imaginative resources are largely neglected during education and devalued in most situations after graduation.[7]

One faith empowering group member confirmed the difficulty he had in freeing his imagination when he commented: "I have been trained to dismiss any idea whose productiveness is not instantly visible!" If people are to live imaginatively into the two horizons of a contemporary personal presentation and an ancient biblical passage, the participants' imagination needs "pump-priming" or "seeding"— and that is what guided meditations can provide.

Our use of guided meditations, however, is not explained wholly by the importance of giving an initial assist to group imagination. Another major reason has to do with the very nature of *biblical interpretation*. Because the meaning of a biblical passage is shaped in significant ways by the horizon of that passage, it is necessary for the interpreter to try to understand that horizon. By helping people enter imaginatively into the horizon of the Bible, the guided meditation helps to interpret scripture.

Many of the details of the horizon of the Bible as a whole, and of its individual passages, are spelled out in biblical commentaries. Before a faith empowering group leader writes a guided meditation, therefore, we strongly encourage that person to read one or more commentaries on the scripture passage selected for a given session.[8] Commentaries can give important context, connotation and background for a given biblical passage, thus filling in important dimensions of the horizon of that passage.

Biblical commentaries make available to people the distilled wisdom of biblical criticism, a vast field of scholarly inquiry accumulated over the course of the past century-plus. Such criticism involves painstaking analysis of scripture from various dimensions, including literary, historical, and cultural. The faith empowering process uses biblical criticism as a means to an end—to shed light on the horizon of a biblical passage for a particular guided meditation. Biblical criticism is not used in the six-step process as an end in itself; understanding the details of an horizon is not the same as living imaginatively into that horizon. Yet understanding the details is an important means to an end. If we are to engage a contemporary personal horizon in creative and responsible dialogue with an ancient biblical horizon, it is important to make every effort to understand those horizons as accurately as possible. And commentaries can provide significant, sometimes crucial, help with the horizon of scripture.

Basically, we have found the guided meditations used in faith empowering groups to fall within one of two categories:

A/An attempt to help the faith empowering group to live imaginatively into an *ancient biblical setting;*
B/ An attempt to help the faith empowering group to live imaginatively into *some contemporary reworking of a* biblical *setting.*

Either way, the guided meditation attempts to provide a responsible "bridge" between the personal presentation of step two and the scripture passage of step three—a bridge on which the imagination of the faith empowering group is free to adventure.

Over time we developed some guidelines for the writing of guided meditations:

Guidelines for Guided Meditation Writing

FAITH EMPOWERING GROUPS

1/Let spontaneity and creativity be your guide. There is no one "right way" to do guided meditations!

2/Begin the guided meditation with specific instructions guiding the group to relax, to sit comfortably, and to close their eyes. Focusing on the relaxation of tense muscles can be effective in freeing the imagination.

3/It is also helpful at the beginning of the guided meditation to lead the group into an opening of themselves to the inner life of the spirit. Often this leading can be done along with focusing people's attention on their breathing.

4/After aiding people in relaxing and opening to the life of the spirit, the guided meditation needs to invite them to enter the world of imagination. Usually, the group is invited through imagination to enter a specific scene at a particular time and place.

5/One way to write a guided meditation is to ask group members to imagine that they are a particular character in the *biblical* story—or a *contemporary version* of that story—and to lead them into an imaginative experience of the story through that character.

6/Another effective technique is to guide people in their imagination into an encounter with Jesus and to give people time to enter into the feelings which this encounter inspires.

7/The most effective guided meditations are the sparsest, leading group members to various points along the way where they can be challenged and questioned about how they feel (emotional responses are particularly important), what they see, what they would say or hear, etc. The meditation needs to have enough colorful detail to "hook" people's imagination, yet enough open-endedness to allow free expression of that imagination once it is "hooked."

8/It is important to give people's imaginations *time* to respond to challenges and questions—and most people's imaginations work slowly. Don't be afraid of substantial pauses for silence!

9/Be careful not to lose people once you have taken them down an imaginative path. After taking the group to a "door of multiple options" and giving people the freedom to choose from among those options, don't pick up the thread of the guided meditation with an assumption that everyone has chosen the same option! Respect and plan for the diversity of people's responses to a meditation, as that diversity may well contribute to whatever empowerment in faith may occur.

10/It is usually better to invite people's imaginations to live fully into a single character, than to risk confusing the imagination with invitations to live into multiple perspectives of several characters.

11/Some form of closing is necessary for the guided meditation. In the six-step faith empowering process, the guided meditation comes just before, and leads directly into, the image pooling of step four. We have found through experience that a faith empowering group does image pooling best when group members stay in their relaxed state. Therefore, the closing of the guided meditation usually includes an instruction to the group to stay in their relaxed state, eyes closed, and to share publicly whatever images, feelings or word associations come to mind out of the presenter's sharing, the biblical passage, and the guided meditation.

12/Remember in finishing the content of the guided meditation to leave room for a diversity of imaginative responses. The ending is best left open-ended. Do not try to tie it all together with some conclusion or moral of the leader!

13/It is important at some point to call people gently, but firmly, out of the imaginative world of the guided meditation back to the world where we are living. In the faith empowering process, this calling back is done at the beginning of "step five: making connections—merging horizons" (see chapter seven) but it is mentioned here for reference because of its importance.

14/In creating a guided meditation, some have found it helpful to jot down "uncensored" ideas over the space of a week or so, before sifting out the best ideas for the actual writing.

15/Guided meditations are one way to prime the pump of human imagination. Some people may prefer other forms of pump-priming than creative writing, such as art, music, or drama; or a combination, such as words and music. Experimentation is welcome!

We would encourage faith empowering group leaders to try their hand at writing guided meditations, although we do not believe it is either necessary or wise to build in an expectation that all leaders must do their own. It would be unfortunate if the only factor keeping someone from participating in a faith empowering group were some requirement to write guided meditations! Still, the challenge is an important one to be held out to people. One participant commented that guided meditation writing was "one of the most difficult, infuriating, rewarding, not-to-be-missed experiences" of the whole process! His words have been echoed by many, many others.

The same participant above also commented that the guided meditation "is often (almost always) a *gift* from the leader to the presenter. The meditation written for my presentation was just that for me—and has been rsponsible for many changes in my own life and my search for increased faith." It is largely because of this *gift* character of guided meditations that we *strongly recommend that leaders not share their meditations with the presenter ahead of the actual faith empowering group session.* When the presenter first hears the guided meditation at the same time that the rest of the group does, the freshness of the gift maximizes its empowering potential!

Let us close this section on biblical horizon and guided meditations by giving an example of a guided meditation for illustrative purposes. (We will give a series of examples of guided meditations in chapter thirteen, for those who wish greater elaboration.) The following meditation was written in relation to a personal presentation about anxiety for the future, and in relation to the "lilies of the field" passage of Matthew 6:25–33. That biblical passage begins with Jesus' words from the Sermon on the Mount: "Therefore I tell you, do not be anxious about your life." The guided meditation was as follows:

A Sample Guided Meditation

"THE ANXIETY BAG"—MATTHEW 6:25–33

"Begin, if you will, by relaxing. Put both your feet on the floor. Sit in a position that is comfortable. Close your eyes. Go around inside your body and turn the tension switch on each muscle from 'high' to 'low'—your neck, your shoulders, your back, your arms, your legs, your feet. Breathe in . . . and breathe out. . . . As you breathe in, feel yourself being filled with God's Holy Spirit. . . . As you breathe out, feel the anxieties you have brought with you flow away. . . . Breathe in. . . . Breathe out. . . .

"Now picture yourself in the middle of the busiest moment of your last week. But instead of carrying all of your cares, your worries, your concerns on the inside, imagine that you are carrying all of these in a laundry bag over your back. Each care, each worry, each concern is a brick in that bag. And on the outside of that bag is a bright orange label: ANXIETY. Take a few moments and name the bricks that are in that anxiety bag. . . . Feel the strain in your back, your legs, as you shoulder the weight of the bag. . . .

"As you are standing there, carrying your anxiety bag, you look up and see Jesus coming toward you. What expression do you see on his face? . . . How do you feel about him coming toward you? . . .

"He offers to take ahold of one side of your anxiety bag to share the load. And then, with a warm smile, he invites you to take the bricks out of the bag, one by one. How do you feel about his invitation? . . . Can you obey? Please try! Which bricks do you lift out first? . . .

"At last your anxiety bag is empty. Jesus hands back the corner of the bag that he was holding, and you drape it over your shoulder, standing straight and tall! But, he is not finished. In his hand he holds out a new bag, one that is labeled, KINGDOM OF GOD. What color is the label on this new bag? . . . The bag looks big, and stuffed full. Jesus asks you to carry that bag with him. How do you feel about his request? . . .

"Now it is time to share the feelings, images and word pictures that have come to mind from the presenter's sharing, from the scripture reading, and from this guided meditation. Stay in your relaxed mood with your eyes closed, and, as you are ready, share out loud what images come to your heart and mind. . . ."

6/Imagining and Imaging

STEP 4: POOLING IMAGES. During this step, the presenter listens quietly. The leader invites the rest of the group—still in the mood of relaxed meditation—to share as many images and feelings as possible which come to mind from the biblical passage and guided meditation of step three, and from the personal presentation of step two. The purpose of this sharing is to provide a "pool of images" from which the presenter may draw new insights into both life experience and scripture.

In Luke 16:1–8, Jesus tells a parable about the steward of a rich man who was accused of wasteful management of his master's goods, and fired from his job. Before the steward left that job, however, he "wrote off" portions of the bills that various creditors owed his boss. He acted to make friends for himself while he was still in a position to do so, "so that people may receive me into their houses when I am put out of the stewardship" (verse 4). Jesus concludes: "The master commended the dishonest steward for his prudence; for the [children] of this world are wiser in their own generation than the [children] of light" (verse 8).

We used this parable once as the scripture passage in a faith empowering group session. The leader gave a guided meditation on the passage. And then the group moved into image pooling—spaces of silence punctuated by words or phrases or sentences from various group members. Those members were sharing out loud the images or feelings that came to their minds from the faith empowering session

36

so far. One participant mentioned the name of Michael Caine, the movie actor who often plays the role of a dashing rogue, as her image of the dishonest steward!

As it turned out, that image was particularly helpful to the session's presenter, who had just shared with the group his struggle over his feelings about money. The presenter had received a loan some years ago from a relative, yet the loan rested uneasily with him, because the presenter did not respect the relative, nor the way in which that relative had made his money. But now, in a flash of insight, the presenter realized that the relative also fit the Michael Caine image as a kind of "lovable rogue." The image provided a fresh perspective from which the presenter could find new meaning in a difficult relationship and a difficult history.

Such is some of the promise and potential of this fourth step of the faith empowering process. Two horizons have been sketched out already in the process—a personal horizon in step two and a biblical one in step three. A preliminary imaginative link has been forged between those horizons through a guided meditation. Now the task for the group is to fill up an "imaginative pool" with as many images as possible—images which the presenter may be able to use to connect the two horizons and to search for new meaning and insight for his or her personal experience and for Scripture.

Image pooling is not a contest to see who can come up with the best or the cleverest word picture. The image of Michael Caine above was only one of a number of images thrown out by the group into a verbal "pool." Some of the other images may well have been more imaginative, more brilliant, more adventuresome. The point, however, was that the image of the movie actor rogue happened to be the one that "clicked" with the presenter. Since the group has only a sketchy idea in advance of which images may, or may not, "click," the group's task is to brainstorm images freely from every possible angle, in the hope that at least a few may be valuable to the presenter. It is not a question of each member worrying whether her ideas will be chosen, or his ideas rejected; members simply offer whatever comes to the surface within their mind or heart as they live into the two horizons, and hope that the presenter will find something of value.

Another example may be helpful here. In one faith empowering group session, a group member offered the image of the presenter as a kind of self-directed Pieta, cradling his body in his own arms. The presenter in this image was both the one doing the cradling and the one being cradled. Somehow the combination of both roles in one image was deeply moving to the presenter, who was struggling with inner and outer anxieties at a transitional time in his life.

We believe it is important for the presenter to remain quiet during this step. To participate in articulating images would be to take an active role, and the best stance for the presenter at this point is the more passive stance of listener or recipient of images. In addition, the presenter is already thoroughly familiar with his or her own presentation; any images the presenter would be likely to share at this point in the process would probably grow out of, and be congruent with, his or her own familiar horizon of meaning. If the hope of faith empowering is to enrich or expand the presenter's horizon with new insights, it is important that the presenter be quiet here so that others can offer their differing perspectives.

If the presenter is to remain quiet, he or she can well afford to jot down a few notes on some of the key images which are offered by members of the group. It will be helpful to the presenter later on if she or he has a list of the important images to draw from as the group works with the presenter to make connections between the presenter's personal experience and the scripture lesson.

Step four can well afford a mood of playfulness and humor. Insights can come through laughter, and they may be easier to accept in an open, non-defensive way when they are packaged in humor! The faith empowering process, we believe, is capable of handling the most sacred, serious, and troubling of personal concerns, and yet its mood need not—indeed probably should not—always be heavy. Jesus, himself, used a kind of playfulness and humor in the imagery he chose for his parables; we are following in a good tradition if we take risks in a similar way today.

The pooling of *images* means just that. The faith empowering process works best when group members can move beyond the temptation to share only *ideas and opinions* to the possibility of articulating *images and word pictures*. Step four is not an exercise in rational discourse but rather an adventure in imagination. There is nothing wrong with sharing abstract ideas in this step, but when group members can translate those ideas into vivid images, the presenter's own imagination may be stimulated more creatively into new insights.

We have talked about *imagination* already. But this fourth step immerses us more deeply in that area of human knowing. We can well afford, therefore, a fuller discussion of imagination.

The word can call to mind the term *imaginary*, which when translated to the world of faith would lead us to Mark Twain's reputed
sarcastic cut: "Faith is believing what you know ain't so!" But James
Loder of Princeton, a Christian scholar in the field of imagination,
makes a critical and helpful distinction: "By imagina*tive*, I do not
mean imagin*ary*. The imaginative thought, act, or word puts you into
history; the imaginary takes you out. The imaginative links the
private to the public world, the imaginary is hidden in privacy. God's
action in history can vindicate the imaginative vision; [God's] action
shatters the imaginary."[1]

Clearly, the faith empowering process tries to be *imaginative, not
imaginary.* Our use of imagination is an attempt to put group members "into history"—the history of a contemporary presenter and the
history of scripture. Imagination in the six-step process is used out in
the open, where there is a healthy possibility of linking "the private to
the public world." That linking is done by setting participants' imaginations in dialogue with such "partners" as biblical passages and
commentaries, publicly shared personal experience, and group discussion.

But what of the relationship of imagination and spirituality? Urban
Holmes, an Episcopal priest, wrote that: "Imagination creates perspective, which results from seeing, not apart from the phenomena
but through and beyond the phenomena."[2] Today's secular world
appears to be devoid of the presence of God, he continues, "not
necessarily because God has died, has withdrawn, or has been discovered to be an illusion, but because, among the large majority of
people, that data which would lead us to conclude God is present in
our experience is quite unconsciously, but effectively, not seen."[3]

We believe that *a large part of the reason why society may feel that
God is not there is because society may have lost much of its imagination, and along with it much of the power of faith.* The eyes of faith
may well depend on the eyes of imagination! Samuel Taylor Cole-
ridge, the English poet, wrote some time ago that the human is most
true to its own nature when the powers of imagination are fully
awake, for imagination is the activity of spirit, "the breath of the
power of God."[4] And, more recently, Jesuit William Lynch wrote
words of power to a world desperate for lasting hope: "The possibility of change is identical with hope itself. Where there is no hope,
or very little, it is because the imagination is literally stuck or trapped
and cannot change its images. . . . Faith is a form of imagining and
experiencing the world."[5]

"The imagination is literally stuck or trapped and cannot change its images. . . ." That quote is a good description of the state of mind of many a person as he or she wrestles with a stubborn piece of personal experience. And the quote also describes why many a person in the role of presenter might want to bring that piece of personal experience to a faith empowering group. The person whose imagination is stuck wants it freed.

The process of freeing the imagination in step four is not that complicated. One person in the group mentions an image. And that image stimulates a new image or a variation on a theme in another person. And so it goes. . . . One person mentions the image of bread. Another thinks of Jesus breaking and distributing bread to the five thousand around him (Mark 6:30–44). Another thinks of Communion. Still another leaps in imagination to a contemporary party where someone lifts his glass to toast the guest of honor. . . . Imagination creates its own expanding avenues of adventure, and each new image carries with it the possibility of new insight for the presenter.

This fourth step, the pooling of images, often provides the greatest hope in the faith empowering process for freeing that which is stuck. There are, as we have stated before, no guarantees in any finite process that faith will be empowered. It is God's Holy Spirit, we must remember, who finally does the empowering, and that Spirit cannot be programmed: "The wind blows where it wills, and you hear the sound of it, but you do not know whence it comes or whither it goes; so it is with every one who is born of the Spirit" (John 3:8). Still, the pooling of images can give the Spirit an abundance of material to work with in trying to pry the imagination out of its ruts. And the more the Spirit has to work with, the more hope there is of a liberated imagination.

Image pooling can be hard work. It can be difficult work, because, paradoxically, it is more like *play* than work, and many of us in this busy, modern world are sadly too unfamiliar with real play. Image pooling was the hardest step of the six-step process for us to figure out, then to describe, and finally to make effective. And yet, once we have gotten a handle on what we were trying to do, this step has become more and more natural, and valuable.

What we are trying to do in step four, quite simply, is to tap the diverse resources of group imagination for the empowering of the presenter's faith. Why? Urban Holmes gives a reason for such an effort, and a reason in general for our substantial use of imagination in the faith empowering process: "If the church is to be open to the presence of God in Christ now, it has to live a life of imagination."[6]

7/Making Connections

STEP 5: MAKING CONNECTIONS—MERGING HORIZONS. The leader checks with the presenter to see if he or she has enough images, feelings, associations, and insights to work with fruitfully. If not, the group continues the pooling of images a while longer. If so, the leader invites the group to come out of its meditative state, and the presenter to rejoin the conversation. The leader then helps the presenter and the rest of the group to work in partnership to focus the points of connection between the presenter's personal presentation, the Bible passage, and the guided meditation, and to probe the meaning of those connections.

It is critical in this fifth step of the faith empowering process for the presenter to join the conversation as an *active participant and partner.* Just as it was important for the presenter to remain quiet during step four in order to maximize the possibility of fresh insight, so is it important for the presenter to participate actively in step five as the group probes the possible meanings of any new insights. Faith empowering is *not* a process in which a group of people do the work *for* the presenter, but rather a process in which a supportive group works *with* the presenter towards the goal of empowering that presenter's faith. This goal of *working with* is best respected if the presenter is an active participant in step five's exploration for new meaning.

The leader closes step four by asking the presenter if he or she has heard enough insightful new images for a potentially creative and helpful discussion. If the presenter has not yet heard anything particularly new or useful, he or she can ask the group to continue its image pooling for a while longer. But it is the hope of the faith empowering process that within some reasonable period of time (we have found *fifteen minutes* to be generally ample for group image pooling) the presenter will feel, and respond, that enough creative images have been offered in step four that it is timely for the group to move to step five.

When the presenter gives the go-ahead, the leader needs to call the faith empowering group out of the relaxed, eyes-closed state that that group has been in since the reading of the guided meditation in step three. Such "calling out" (as we mentioned in chapter five) needs to be done gently but firmly by the leader, allowing time for group members to make the necessary mental and spiritual transition from one spiritual state to another. It may be helpful for the leader to remind the group briefly *what it has done so far* in that particular session, to recall for the group *where it is* in the six-step process, and to *restate the goal* of that session as the *empowering of a particular presenter's faith*. Such reminders underscore the need and importance of facilitating a clear transition from relaxed imagination to group discussion, and are particularly crucial in the earlier stages of a faith empowering group's formation.

Then the leader needs to invite the presenter to initiate the discussion of step five. This invitation openly brings the presenter back into active participation in the process. It also allows the presenter the freedom to choose what she would most like to pursue with the group, or what he would prefer to set aside; the presenter may well choose to by-pass some of the images pooled by the group as irrelevant to that presenter's particular faith journey or as images better considered at a later time in private, and such by-passing is fully permissible. The leader simply asks the presenter here to name two or three group images that seem to be particularly helpful to him or her and that the presenter would like to discuss and explore in more depth with the group.

Once the presenter has initiated step five by highlighting a few images that appear worthy of further exploration, the leader may stand back a bit for the duration of step five and let the presenter take the lead in the discussion. If the presenter becomes the focus in step five, as we affirm, the leader's role for a time becomes that of "process watchdog" or "gatekeeper of the process," helping to insure that the group is trying to work *with and not for* the presenter, that the group is not slipping into the temptation of trying to give advice or answers or solutions to the presenter, and that group members are listening well to each other. In addition, the leader must help participants to resist the temptation to wander off into their own issues by guiding

them back to focus on the presenter. Finally, the leader needs to be
sensitive to that time when step five has gone as far as it can helpfully
go for the presenter. When that point has been reached, the leader
needs to step back into the role of discussion leader and move the
group to the final step of the process.

We need to say more here about the goal of the discussion in step
five. If the group is trying to empower the presenter's faith, how do
we understand that such empowering happens? And, if the group is
not trying to give advice, answers or solutions, what is it trying to
do? To answer these questions we need to explore our understanding
of biblical interpretation.

Biblical Interpretation Theory

The theory of biblical interpretation is at once a challenging and an
important discipline. We believe it is valuable to include a section on
such theory in this book, though we recognize that different readers
will have different levels of interest in the intricacies of that theory.

We have twice quoted Hans-Georg Gadamer's description of an
horizon as "the range of vision that includes everything that can be
seen from a particular vantage point."[1] And, under our descriptions
of *personal horizon* and *biblical horizon,* we have elaborated an understanding of an "horizon of meaning" to include the personal,
cultural, historical, psychological, scientific, and sociological elements that can be "seen" (heard, felt, smelled, or tasted) from a
particular point in space and time.

How do these two horizons—the contemporary and the scriptural—relate to each other?[2] Again, borrowing from Gadamer, we
may begin an answer to this question by focusing on two concepts of
interpretation theory: *distance* and *fusion.*

First, *distance.* Distance is the recognition that there is a gap
between the sandal-wearing, demon-believing world of ancient Palestine, and the mass-marketed, computerized world of contemporary
America. Distance is the awareness that the context of healing which
we take for granted today—intensive care units, drug therapy, and the
latest electronic equipment—was unheard of when people brought
the sick to Jesus. Distance is the realization that the problems of
world peace in a nuclear age are far more complex than the problems
of such a vision in an age when people literally hoped to "beat their
swords into plowshares" (Isaiah 2:4).

There may well be times when the interpreter can ignore the

distance between the biblical and contemporary horizons without seriously affecting that interpreter's work. One thinks, for example, of the time when Jesus gave new importance to Leviticus 19:18 as his second great commandment: "You shall love your neighbor as yourself" (March 12:31). We could well argue that the fundamental meaning of that commandment is not substantially altered by the changed horizon of the term "neighbor" from the first century to the twentieth; the horizon of neighbor is far larger in today's interconnected world, but the commandment to love is essentially unchanged.

In passages such as the second great commandment above, the biblical interpreter may well deny that there are any differences between the contemporary and biblical horizons which are all that significant for our life of faith. Spending a lot of time and energy analyzing the distance between horizons would be largely irrelevant to the basic point Jesus was trying to make. All one has to do to understand scripture in this case is to let the message of the Bible speak directly to the person of today.

But, we believe, not every passage of scripture can be related to contemporary life so simply and directly. Nor can every area of modern life be related simply and directly to a relevant biblical passage. Sooner or later, the interpreter must come to grips with the real distance between biblical and contemporary horizons.

At this point, we need to affirm that *distance* is not necessarily negative, as one might suspect. To say that the biblical horizon has its distance from our modern horizon does not, for example, necessarily assert the irrelevance of the biblical. Gadamer writes: "In fact the important thing is to recognise the distance in time as a positive and productive possibility of understanding."[3] The distance between the biblical age and the modern age can help us to *recognize the blind spots* in the *horizons* of *both ages.* And with the advantage of this understanding of blind spots, there is less of a chance that we may stumble and fall unawares.

We may look here at an example of what we believe to be a blind spot in the horizon of the modern world: The psalmist *of old* could write: "The earth is the Lord's and the fulness thereof" (Psalm 24:1a). The biblical horizon included the belief that the earth belonged to God. The horizon of our *modern* world, however, is more likely to assume that the earth "belongs" to the nations, groups, and individuals who "own" its pieces, rather than to God. Is there not a blind spot here in today's secular view of life, a blind spot that may be directly related to our modern ecological failures at exercising appropriate

stewardship of the earth's natural resources? Rather than looking at
the earth as a whole, do we not get trapped into a concern for only
those pieces of the earth that we "own," and a failure to be concerned
with what we do not "own"? If there is a blind spot here, does not
our recognition of it focus attention on an important area for remedial
action?

Blind spots may exist in our modern horizon, *but they may also be
present in the biblical horizon.* We are not stating here that the biblical
Word itself is untrue. We are stating, however, that the biblical
horizon within which that Word was originally proclaimed may well
be wrong or inadequate. The standard of judgment for such a statement can be the biblical Word itself, as that Word is fully revealed in
Jesus Christ. It is not our contemporary horizon that serves as the
standard for judging the biblical horizon, but the God who was
revealed in Christ. And yet, the differences between the contemporary and biblical horizons can make us aware of the inadequacies of
the latter.

One thinks, for example, of the Genesis passage so often quoted in
wedding services: "Therefore a man leaves his father and his mother
and cleaves to his wife" (Genesis 2:24). That passage emphasizes the
need for the husband-to-be to leave his parents but, coming from a
different culture than ours, it does not speak of the similar need for
the wife-to-be to do such leaving. Today's American culture, however, is moving towards an understanding of marriage as a covenant of
equals, in which it is as important for the *woman to leave her father
and mother* as it is for the *man to leave his*—so that they both can
cleave to each other. One contemporary wedding service, for example, "calls both man and woman to leave their parents in order to be
fully united with each other." That insight into marriage as a covenant
of equals between male and female is ultimately rooted in the new
humanity that Christ brings to all of us, regardless of our sex (Gala-
tians 3:28). Yet it may well be that our contemporary horizon, with
its focus on the goal (though not yet the reality) of equality of
opportunity for both sexes, may lead us to an awareness of the blind
spot of sexism which exists in the biblical horizon.

Another example of the inadequacy of the biblical horizon can be
seen in the imagery in Psalm 51:7: "Wash me, and I shall be whiter
than snow." The psalmist is talking about God's forgiving and healing
love, which is as true today as it was in biblical times. Yet the imagery
for that love uses a particular color, white, and the implications of that
color are exclusive in our multi-racial society. Black people, for

example, could hardly assert that they would be "whiter than snow" when washed. Yet Black is as beautiful as white. The Word of forgiveness needs to be retained, but the horizon in which that Word was expressed is inadequate for the full truth of God's forgiving love for all races of the world as we see that love in Jesus Christ.

A third example has to do with biblical passages which are critical of Jews in what Christians call the Old Testament. Within the biblical horizon, these passages need to be understood as *self*-criticism. When Amos, for example, spoke of the transgressions of Judah and Israel (Amos 2:4–8) he was speaking as a member of the household of faith to other members of that same household, seeking their common reformation. However, it is quite another thing for the Christian tradition to use these same texts to condemn Judaism and avoid the very self-correction such passage could enable. The same point could be made of a passage of Christian scripture such as Matthew 22:1–14. When Jesus talked about inviting guests to a marriage feast, he was speaking as a Jew to Jews. When Christians today, who live in the same generation as the Nazi Holocaust, interpret the parable as a story about the inacceptability of Jews, we participate in irreparable harm not only to Jews, but to the core message of the gospel of love, for which Jesus gave his life.

One factor which is important in biblical interpretation, then, is to hope for the positive goal of increased understanding through awareness of blind spots in the two horizons, scriptural and contemporary. To realize that goal, it is necessary to bring those two horizons into dynamic interrelationship with each other. It is necessary to seek (as our second concept of interpretation theory puts it) a *fusion* or *merging of horizons*.

If Gadamer could write about the positive value of recognizing *distance* between two horizons, he also can write about the complementary value of *fusion*: "The horizon of the present cannot be formed without the past. There is no more an isolated horizon of the present than there are historical horizons. Understanding, rather, is always the fusion of these horizons which we imagine to exist by themselves."[4] When our modern horizon merges or fuses with the horizon of a biblical author, we are able to transcend our differences in a way that enables the insights of that distant author to become our own.

An analogy might help. The biblical horizon is like a single lens, and the modern horizon is similar to a second lens. The distance between the two horizons allows for focus and depth perception in the same way that the distance between the lenses of our two eyes allows for such focus. And the fusion or merging of horizons is equivalent to the common focus of the two lenses.

Distance and fusion together make responsible understanding possible. Distance without fusion would contribute to a sense that the Bible has little relevance to life today. And fusion without distance could leave us with a distorted or oversimplified view of what relevance the Bible actually does have. Distance plus fusion can highlight the prejudices and blind spots of each horizon in a way that can help us to understand what we have to avoid or overcome. Biblical interpretation by itself does not heal the blind spots, but at least it makes us aware of what needs to be healed.

We have been dependent on the work of Hans-Georg Gadamer for much of our analysis above. To be fair to him, we should note here that his own purpose has been "not to develop a procedure of understanding, but to clarify the conditions in which understanding takes place."[5] The six-step faith empowering process is rooted, we believe, in Gadamer's understanding of biblical interpretation. Yet, as a "process" or "procedure of interpretation," it goes beyond the particular limits Gadamer set for himself.

How does the six-step faith empowering process build on Gadamer's insights into the nature of biblical interpretation? The *distance* between the contemporary personal horizon of step two and the ancient biblical horizon of step three is affirmed by a number of factors. The selection in the preparation session of scripture that is not too close to the personal presentation affirms that distance. So, too, does the use of biblical commentaries as background for the writing of a guided meditation help people to understand and live into the unique dimensions of the horizon of a biblical passage. And the discontinuity or break between step two, the sharing of the personal presentation, and step three, the reading of scripture, can give the faith empowering group a feel for the distance between the two horizons.

The complementary importance of *fusing or merging horizons* is also affirmed in the faith empowering process. The purpose of the guided meditation as an "imaginative bridge" between horizons helps to begin the work of fusion. The pooling of images continues that work by providing further imaginative links between horizons. And the fifth step of "making connections—merging horizons" is designed to solidify that fusion work. In step five the goal is to explore and to name some of the ways the group's imagination may have made possible a new merging of horizons between contemporary experience and the world of the Bible.

Step five is not an attempt to "distill" the message of the Bible out from its ancient horizon in order to be able to render that message intelligible to the modern world. Such an effort at "distillation" is the goal, for example, of Rudolph Bultmann's famous method of biblical interpretation: demythologizing.[6] Step five is rather an attempt to bring the *whole* biblical horizon of a particular passage (not the essential message behind that horizon) into creative dialogue with the *whole* contemporary horizon of an individual presenter. The goal is to make connections between those horizons of meaning, not to try to express the meaning of one in terms that make sense within the other.

The tasks of living imaginatively into two horizons, and seeking ways to merge those horizons, are tasks that take all the rational, intellectual abilities we can bring to them. But they are also tasks which call on all of the emotional, aesthetic, sensory, and intuitive abilities we can use as well.

Philosopher Paul Ricoeur names the attitude which is appropriate for these tasks a "second naïveté."[7] We all know people who are naïve because they cannot be anything else, naïve because they haven't yet brought their rational, critical faculties to bear on what they are experiencing. A "second naïveté," however, is a naïveté out of choice. It would include the mind with all its critical powers, yet without giving veto power to that mind. A "second naïveté" is the adult capacity to appreciate a good story for what it is worth, recognizing whatever limitations it may have, yet appreciating its value as story nonetheless. It is this adult capacity which we seek to tap in challenging a faith empowering group to make connections between a presenter's horizon and a biblical horizon.

If step five of the faith empowering process is empowering, it is because the simple act of forging imaginative links between two distant horizons really can lead, we believe, to the merging of those horizons. And as the horizons are merged, the meanings and power of each can flow into the other. In the six step process, imagination and biblical interpretation join together in seeking to empower the presenter's faith.

Two Examples of Making Connections

One person gave a presentation expressing a sense of meaninglessness about a present vocation—meaninglessness in spite of long training and experience. The mood was one of anxiety and risk in admitting such meaninglessness, but also a preliminary hint of adventure in the possibility, however dimly envisioned, of new fulfillment.

The biblical passage selected for that faith empowering session was the story of the rich young ruler, who asks Jesus, "Good Teacher, what shall I do to inherit eternal life?" (Luke 18:18) When Jesus responds by listing some of the ten commandments, the man replies that he has always followed those.

> And when Jesus heard it, he said to him, "One thing you still lack. Sell all that you have and distribute to the poor, and you will have treasure in heaven; and come, follow me." But when he heard this he became sad, for he was very rich. (Luke 18:22–23)

There are clear differences between the contemporary world of work with its technological sophistication and the ancient world. There is also an element of distance between the contemporary welfare system which would care for someone who sold all that he had, and the ancient world which had no such system. Yet the horizons of the personal presentation and the biblical passage do merge or fuse, nonetheless. Both vocation and wealth are symbols of security. To risk giving them up is to risk both anxiety and freedom. And to take that risk requires faith as trust. In relating the story of vocational meaninglessness and the story of the rich young ruler, the faith empowering group could gain fresh insight into the burden of critical decision-making when faith is at risk.

* * *

Another presenter talked of the difficulty of preserving an emotional balance to work effectively within the minute-to-minute time pressures of a demanding job. "My 'churn index,'" he said, "records the internal pressures that in times past build to ulcers or tension headache." He struggled with his job responsibilities, his church-related activities, and the tension between planning his time and being open to the multiple intrusions of people who had legitimate claims on that time.

The faith empowering group placed this personal presentation in dialogue with the story of Jesus and the paralytic lowered through the roof (Mark 2:1–12). In the middle of one of Jesus' sermons, four men lowered a paralytic down from the roof into Jesus' presence, hoping that their handicapped friend might be healed.

There are clear differences between a contemporary job-holder and Jesus of Nazareth, though we affirm that the church's long-standing conviction that Jesus was fully human (the church also affirms that Jesus was fully divine) does not render illegitimate a discussion which places a contemporary presenter in a position which is analogous, in part, to Jesus. What the faith empowering group noted, however, was that Jesus probably experienced his own "churn index" at the moment his sermon was interrupted by a paralytic lowered through the roof. There is room for creative dialogue between a busy modern jobholder and Jesus in his ministry at just the point of how each may cope with unplanned intrusions in the midst of other important agenda.

8/*Drawing Implications*

STEP 6: CLOSING SHARING AND PRAYER. The leader invites each group member, including the presenter, to share whatever personal implications or directions for the future the session may have brought to light. Each person is to share the session's implications for herself or himself, and is free to share—or not to share—whatever she or he wishes. The leader then offers the experience of that faith empowering group meeting to God in prayer.

When the discussion of step five has run its course, the faith empowering group leader needs to move the group to the sixth and final step. Here the leader invites any group member who so wishes to describe briefly whatever implications the session may have had for him or her. This is not an invitation for a participant to try to articulate the implications the session might be expected to have for the presenter; if the presenter wants to articulate those implications for herself, that is good, but others should not try to speak for the presenter (as we have asserted throughout the above discussion). Each group member, rather, is invited here to express whatever implications that group member himself may have drawn from the session, and may be willing to share with the group.

Step six is clearly an attempt to broaden the focus of the session from the presenter to the group as a whole. It gives all group members a chance to reflect briefly on the major implications the session may have had for them. Yet, such group reflection may have an empowering side effect for the presenter, as well. Often, group members will articulate insights or implications for them which reveal or confirm that "they are in the same boat" as the presenter. It can be

empowering for the presenter to realize once again that he or she is
not alone.

The leader in step six would do well to push the group to articulate
implications *for action* as well as the more reflective insights they may
have found. The six-step process needs to feed back into the rest of
life, and not become some isolated and reflective intermission, if it is
to be truly empowering.

Lawrence LeShan, an author in the field of meditation, underscores
the importance of pushing meditative insights into plans for action:

> The belief that "enlightenment" occurs suddenly and completes the whole task
> when it happens is curiously similar to the belief in "insight" in the early days
> of psychotherapy. . . . Alas. Long hard experience in psychotherapy has taught
> us that this is not so. True, insight experiences fitting the description occur (as
> do enlightenment experiences), but they are only the beginning. They, by
> themselves, rarely change much. After insight comes the long hard work of
> following it up: of changing our perceptions, feelings and behavior to gradu-
> ally, painfully, bring them into accord with our understanding.[1]

The faith empowering process, similarly, may provide new insight
and expanded horizons, but it must be followed by long hard work if
such new understanding is to be integrated fully in an empowering
way into the presenter's life.

We may put Lawrence LeShan's point, in relation to faith empowering, another way: *new insight needs to be integrated through
new ministry*—and here we are talking about ministry as the vocation
both of the laity and the clergy. The new insights of faith which may
be found through the faith empowering process can only be owned as
they issue in new actions which express that faith.

The leader closes step six, and the whole faith empowering session,
with prayer. Some of that prayer may be written out in advance or
borrowed from another source, but we would encourage the leader,
as we do in step one, to risk spontaneous prayer for at least a part of
what is said. Spontaneous prayer allows for some direct and immediate lifting up to God of the experience just passed. Some leaders have
opened up the closing prayer to the spontaneous participation of the
group as a whole, inviting any who would like to pray out loud or
silently to do so; the leader would then offer the final spoken words
of that prayer.

The closing prayer is important. Significant experiences may well
have happened—to the presenter and/or others—sometimes without
the group's full awareness. People may well have taken important
risks, felt intense emotion, or experienced deep pain or joy. The faith

empowering process does raise people's expectations, and the actual experience of that process may well mean that some are met and some are not. The group may have been supportive, or fallen short. And faith may have been—or may be in the process of becoming—empowered. All of this experience is well offered up to God's Holy Spirit for healing, renewing, and confirming. In this closing prayer we recall again that it is that Spirit which is the final source of whatever empowering of faith may occur.

> Holy One, You have been with us this day, whether we have felt your presence or not. You have been with us as comforter, healer, challenger. You have held us in love even as you have led us out into more faithful directions. May the experience of this time continue to nourish our lives together and apart. And may we be empowered to serve you afresh in your broken world, even through Jesus Christ, our Lord. Amen.

*   *   *

A time of sociability usually follows a faith empowering session. This "nineteenth hole" can give group members an opportunity to pursue ideas or feelings from the more formal part of the meeting, but without the structure of a process that has such well-defined steps. Many is the time that the value of a group session has not fully emerged until two or three pursue a particular point in a corner of the kitchen over a post-meeting cup of coffee.

9/The Preparation Session

Each faith empowering group needs an enabler who will meet in advance of every faith empowering session for that group with the presenter and leader for that session. We have found it best if the enabler is not a participating member in the faith empowering group itself. These preparation sessions, which are critical to the success of faith empowering groups, are intended to hear and focus the presenter's sharing, to select a relevant biblical passage for that sharing, and to review the leadership needs and possibilities for the particular leader of the session.

The above summary of the goal of the preparation session is fairly straightforward in its statement of the three basic tasks expected. We may elaborate briefly on these tasks:

1. *To hear and focus the presenter's sharing.* The enabler and the leader simply ask the presenter to share what he or she is thinking about presenting at a future faith empowering session. Then, the enabler and leader may probe the material shared, reflecting back to the presenter what they are hearing and feeling, with the hope of helping to focus that presenter's presentation as needed. The presenter may come with a question as to the appropriateness of particular material for a faith empowering presentation, and that question deserves a response (enablers and leaders are referred here to the discussion above under "Step 2: Personal Horizon," and particularly to the Guidelines for Personal Presentations in chapter four). The enabler and the leader may wish to encourage the presenter to decide which of several possible issues she would most like to share, to risk becom-

ing more personal and less "arm's length" in his presentation, or to reach for a deeper sharing in order to make possible a deeper empowerment in faith. The preparation session is a good time to do that encouraging and to work with the presenter in determining how far the presenter wants to go, and is able to go, in responding to such encouragement.

2. *To select a relevant biblical passage for that sharing.* We have discussed the selection of scripture for faith empowering sessions under "Step 3: Biblical Horizon" above in chapter five. It is obviously helpful here if those who are serving as enablers have some familiarity with a range of biblical passages for possible selection, and/or some familiarity with such research tools as a concordance (which lists alongside every word in the Bible all of the biblical verses in which that word is used). The key here, we believe, however, after looking at technical resources, is to trust intuition.

3. *To review the leadership needs and possibilities for the particular leader of the session.* It is helpful for the enabler to run through the six steps of the faith empowering process with the leader, particularly when that leader is relatively new to that process. (Leaders may want to take a faith empowering process summary sheet with them to the group meeting for quick reference—see chapter two.) The enabler should discuss the opening community building question or exercise with both leader and presenter (see the discussion of "Step 1: Sharing and Prayer" above in chapter three). The leader may need help in writing a guided meditation, or may want someone else to write that guided meditation for him or her; the enabler needs to provide that help or arrange for it. And the leader may need assistance from the enabler in the leading of group prayer (see discussions above under "Step 1: Sharing and Prayer" and "Step 6: Closing Sharing and Prayer"—chapters three and eight).

It is best if the preparation session take place at least several days before the actual faith empowering group meeting. It takes time to consult biblical commentaries and to plan and write guided meditations. In addition, the presenter may profit from some time to digest the preparation session before having to share a final presentation with the whole group.

We have found that preparation sessions usually take an hour or so. We have often held these preparation sessions over breakfast—a convenient time for three often busy people to schedule an hour meeting.

We believe it is best that the enabler for a given group not be a regular member of that same group. It can be confusing to the dynamics of the process if one person who knows the presenter's presentation, the opening community building exercise, and the scripture passage—all from the preparation session—tries also to approach the actual faith empowering group session with the same fresh openness that the other group members bring. The enabler who wants to participate in a faith empowering group is well advised, we believe, to join a separate group, and to find another enabler for that group, rather than try to be both enabler and participant in the same group.

Another problem involved in the enabler's meeting with the group may occur if the enabler is a clergyperson and the group is composed of laity. Some laity are so used to deferring to the clergy for "answers" in terms of faith—and some clergy are so used to being deferred to for such "answers"—that the group might become dependent on the clergy-enabler rather than seeking its own empowering. Our experience indicates that laity are beautifully capable of performing all of the roles of faith empowering groups (as, too, are clergy). One of the values of such groups can be the value of lay people discovering their own gifts in relation to faith and spirituality. Such discovery is not intended as a replacement for the gifts of the clergy, but can be aimed towards a greater empowerment of the gifts of the whole church, which is composed of both clergy and laity.

Enablers may also want to sponsor—or see that someone else sponsors—whole group experiences to supplement the life of faith empowering groups. (By "whole group," we mean all of the members of all of the faith empowering groups in a given setting.) Workshops in guided meditation writing, retreats focused on spirituality, education around the Bible and scriptural interpretation—these are only a few examples of the kind of supplementary whole group meetings that might be possible and valuable.

Enablers could well be ordained clergy, but our experience has indicated that lay people can perform that role as well. The role of enabler requires: some sensitivity to the hopes, needs, and risks that a presenter and leader may experience; some familiarity with the faith empowering process, both its theory and its practice; some basic familiarity with the Bible; and some openness to the life of the Spirit, within which the empowering of faith finds its context.

10/The Meaning Behind the Method

What is the meaning of all this? Obviously, the import for partici- pants has varied. For the sake of credibility, we gathered some nine five-year veterans in the process, and asked them to testify personally to the meaning of this experience. A verbatim transcript follows shortly.

The meanings, however, are more than personal. They participate in the broader experience of the nature of faith. Some theories and assumptions about faith development, education, and imagination underscore the faith empowering process. Thomas Groome's "Shared Praxis" approach,[1] and Walter Wink's *The Bible in Human Transformation*,[2] are important examples of theory which we believe is congruent with our process. For those wishing a fuller theoretical treatment than contained here, our Doctor of Ministry dissertation for Andover Newton Theological School is a source,[3] giving our particular blend of theory and practice.

We have already looked into imagination briefly in this book in chapter six, and biblical interpretation in chapter seven. But what can we say about faith development? What can we share from the particular horizon of the faith seeker? What is coming together here? What can we as human beings understand of but one attempt to empower faith? First, a word from some participants in the process.

Interview with Nine Faith Empowering Group Members

Joe: "You have all been in faith empowering groups for five years. How would you describe any growth or change in your life as a result?"

Paul: "What I've gained is a personal understanding of some of the things lots of people had talked about, but I had not experienced; this is the common thread. It has been a way to make faith more real, to see the workings of the Holy Spirit. That sounds trite, perhaps, but I really believe my faith empowering group did this for me over and over again. It increased my recognition of God's grace in a way not available to me before. It increased my ability to take risks, for example, stepping out and completely changing my risk structure, like serving as moderator of the church (although that risk may not have been too great). I am now appreciative of the way God works through people. Maybe that's one of the strongest feelings. It has increased my appreciation of the relationship of the Bible to daily life, a profound experience for me. I would love to find a way to open this process up to new members."

Bill: "In a pastoral call I had this week, a church member said he thought he was now ready for something like a faith empowering group, though he had not been in years past."

Sybil: "And someone expressed interest to me this week as well!"

Doug: "One of the things that occurred to me regarding change is that I am more open to others' lives—to share and to listen. The group I have been in has given some substance to the whole notion of Christian love. I begin to sense what that is all about. I have gained some understanding of the value of a support system, and why it is needed. I am open to others in desperate need of support systems. In my work in the ministry of the laity this need too often rises in consciousness and then disappears."

Sybil: "I think of some very concrete things. An awareness of the Bible as a resource. Before, I had no real sense of a tie there, or what I might have to do with it. I am aware and willing to bear public witness that I need it and use it. I have behaviors now, and an approach to being alive which I did not have five years ago. I feel closer to other people in sharing the love of God. I have more courage in handling potentially conflict-producing situations. I am less defensive, less worried. What will come, will come—the other person and I will be okay. I attribute this to confidence in faith. I'm also not entirely clear on this, but I am more able to talk to God. I'm a person who daydreams a lot, not always quite consciously. Sometimes these are 'kind of' conversations with God. My experience has led me to encounter issues or concerns in my life safely, which otherwise I might have avoided."

Bill: "Can you give examples?"

Sybil: "The opportunity to share fears, angers, personal baggage. When I returned from the Holy Land I was moved and conflicted, and terrified of talking. Other times I would not have thought about talking it out, but I did in our group. My closeness to Don has also been enhanced by being in the same group."

Dorothy: "It has made a difference for me very specifically in my work. The part I've enjoyed most is working with the hospital staff. I work primarily with very young female nurses, who find their work often to be emotionally trying. It always takes a lot of patience. Since my faith empowering participation, I sense I am directed to do that. I sometimes go beyond what my colleagues feel is necessary. Some of that is clarified as a result of our faith empowering group, which offers a range of tools for people's adult faith and development. My nurses have to confront death constantly, which brings in their own personal losses, so they may become very conflicted at work. It is easy for me to justify my investment in these nursing colleagues, occasionally even saying my faith directs me to do this. I feel I am directed to do this."

Sue: "One thing for me has been that the scriptures used in faith empowering sessions have become very personal touchstones which hold me personally in dealing with pieces of my life not solved or done. I see them living there very personally. The choice of scriptures and the presentations I have made have continued to speak importantly to me."

Don: "That has also been a very strong part for me, the nuances that come from scripture. The woman at the well (John 4:7–15) and the house built on the sand (Matthew 7:24–27) come right to mind. The quite remarkable thing is that a faith-oriented approach to a problem may be much the same each time. Yet, I celebrate that, for it has never become stale. The greatest reward is that I have been able to deal with stress with *more* (notice I used a relative term) calmness!"

Dorothy: "I don't think I deal any differently with stress now than I did before, except that I say to myself, wait until I tell them (the faith empowering group) about *this! Then* it will be better. I know there is a place to go with my stress."

Don: "The faith empowering process was very pivotal in my decision to change my employment situation."

Doug: "Paul mentioned his awareness of the Holy Spirit. To me this has been very real. Of course, in certain sessions this goes either up or down. But there have been times when I have been positive that the Holy Spirit is a reality. Not the Holy Ghost as some abstraction."

Marsha: "I would agree with that."

Faye: "I would have to echo so many things others have said. One of the most striking things for me when I first started was the level of trust that was almost immediate: the level of sharing without reservation or fear, in a faith that this would be accepted. For example, later when I took on the opportunity to become vice moderator of the church, the group supported me all the way. Another thing is writing your own guided meditations. This opened up a whole world of resources to me. There were times when I wanted to call the ministers for help, but I didn't, and doing it by myself was very important."

Marsha: "It's difficult to sort out the effects of faith empowering alone, as the last five years have been a time of enormous spiritual growth. It is one of the important things I have been doing, but how much it is responsible for that growth I don't know. I can recall two occasions in particular when I felt God spoke to me. These were times when I presented, and they had deep meaning for me. I can remember clearly one sentence spoken by an individual in my group. One other element we have not touched here yet is that in these groups you give yourself time to focus on a particular issue. The preparation session prior to the group meeting is part of this. Sometimes just the preparation time itself and the focusing resolves the issue. I've heard people say by the time of the meeting itself they no longer feel conflicted."

Dorothy: "And I think that is transferable, as the unconscious significance of the process."

Marsha: "A lot of it is unconscious."

Dorothy: "Setting something aside and openly talking has sometimes changed the way I've looked at things."

Marsha: "The important thing for me, though, is the use of the Bible. I had not used it before. Now it's more a part of my everyday living."

Cindy: "I resonate with that a lot. I can affirm a change in me directly attributable to being in these groups. I'm not aware that there was anything significant before to help me focus on an inner strength or resource. It helps me deal with stress. It feels like a new resource—

not that it always works. But it is a resource that opens me to new creativity and strength."

Sue: "For me it's also the use of imagery. I have been able to use the tool of images to help me a great deal. I have never had that before."

* * *

Bill: "In something like the way we pool our images in an actual faith empowering session, could you share *some images for faith empowering* itself?"

"It's like going to a well."

"Sometimes images in our group meetings come to me, wham, like from an external source!"

"God must have a sense of humor, because a remark will crack us up, and then the images really start to flow."

"I have an image of being encased in armor to ward off blows; a light but important robe."

"I think of a bank account I can go and draw on—going through my mind into a reserve account."

"A life line."

"A safety net."

"A bridge to other people."

"Christmas—receiving the gifts of all the people present."

"A safe harbor."

"An energy source."

"A part of the whole; a building process in which each contributes. You are just a cog."

"It doesn't belong just to the group meeting, either; it extends to changed feelings about new people."

"Like your friend I met in Weston, Vermont, when we visited the Benedictine Priory there, and going on the walk for AIDS."

"It's not just something that happens on Wednesday evenings when we are together—you carry it with you."

"I think of it as an image of Jesus with the tax collectors and sinners. None of us is perfect but it doesn't make much difference."

"I have an image of spiraling and spiraling, like cycles of growth and development and change."

"I have an image of Essie—she keeps coming to mind. Her power. Her fundamental power, like something of a Holy Roller or Shaker. She may say nothing all evening and then she comes out with it. Or she will just start to cry. We held hands and prayed last time at the end, and I swear when Essie poured forth prayer I felt a jolt."

"After our very first meeting, I felt like Peter trying to walk on the water! I had no notion of what we were getting into. At the first go-round it was incomprehensible. One person said as we were leaving the information session, 'This is just too obscure for me.'"

"Once I remember there was no time to prepare, but my presentation fit the scripture like a hand in a glove."

"I image people's ministries to each other, with comfort."

"I have the image of being wrapped in a down comforter."

＊　＊　＊

Bill: "Can you think some more of particular biblical passages that have remained alive for you?"

"Peter walking on the water." (Matthew 14:22-33)

"The energy coming out from Christ, and his knowing when someone had touched his robe." And another: "The woman with the flow of blood." (Luke 8:43-48)

"The cripple outside the gate in Jerusalem." And another: "The man by the pool, whom Jesus tells to heal himself." (John 5:2-9)

"The laborers in the vineyard who complain over their wages." (Matthew 20:1-16)

"The parable of the sower and the seed." (Matthew 13:1-9)

"The calling of Isaiah." (Isaiah 6)

"John's story of the women visiting the tomb and its implications." (John 20:1-18)

"The parable of the talents." (Matthew 25:14-30)

"God searching the far reaches of the earth." (Psalm 139)

"Moses and the burning bush." (Exodus 3)

"The Corinthian passage on spiritual gifts." (1 Corinthians 12)

"Christ in the garden and the disciples asleep." (Matthew 26:36-46)

"The first time Revelation ever made any sense to me: John in the crystal city. What if John didn't want to go?" (Revelation 21)

"An Acts passage of two unlearned people sharing their faith." (Acts 2-4)

"The whole armor of God." (Ephesians 6:11)

"The woman with the jar of perfume." (Matthew 26:6-13)

"The prodigal son." (Luke 15:11-32)

"The raising of Jairus' daughter." (Mark 5:22-24, 35-43)

＊　＊　＊

Bill: "Do you see any limitations to the process at this time?"

"I think maybe it needs something to help some of us now move to a more graduate level. You share deeply your life stories for two years, and then it may need to change. We need more assistance in spiritual disciplines and biblical studies. I am moving beyond the current process, which I don't think itself needs to change."

"We have not always used a personal presentation. We have discussed our feelings about stewardship, about ministry, and what that means in the work place."

"It can be used in different formats, like in ministry of the laity support groups where we used *some* of the steps and a scripture passage."

"I used it once in a budget session of the state conference of our denomination. The budget itself was the personal presentation. Then we went to scripture and guided meditation, and came back to try to make imaginative connections between the budget and the Bible."

"There are other ways to meet spiritual needs on our own, like going to the Weston, Vermont, Priory."

"My outlook is less traditional. I needed the faith empowering exchange to make me stop and listen."

"I do find it limiting to be able to present only once a year. I have a spiritual director, however, and this meets this need."

"It would be enhanced by meeting more than monthly."

"The time *after* the meeting is very important."

"Step 6 is more lengthy in our group now. Someone other than the presenter will say 'There's something going on that I need you all to know,' and we take the time to listen."

* * *

Bill: "Do you have any further reflections on the impact of faith empowering?"

"It has given me solid ground on which to move forward."

"For personal issues, my decisions are made more seriously, with a greater awareness of a spiritual framework."

"At work, it has an almost daily impact. I feel directed, not so wildcat; I feel more purpose, less sense of waste. I take extra time, and feel that this is not falling on barren ground. Others will understand and go on."

"Like stones in the water?"

"No, more like a cycle growing and expanding horizontally, part of something moving forward. Others will stop and think. The tone grows. Like the housekeeper on our unit at work, who just said 'It's a wonderful family we have here.' "

*   *   *

Bill: "There have been two recurring criticisms of faith empowering groups. First is that it might be a comfortable 'parlor game,' simply making us feel good as we sit talking in living rooms, without helping to change the world towards greater social justice. Second is that the faith empowering process may not be able to handle responsibly all of the high-powered, occasionally deeply threatening, issues of human brokenness that presenters might bring to it. How do you feel about these criticisms?"

"Well, it certainly is a personal group, that is centered inward. And yes, very early on, our group came close to being in very deep water. It was critical for us to realize that our purpose was *not to solve; not to analyze each other.*"

"It has been the first time in my life that I've been in a group that has addressed serious faith issues in more than just an academic way. The void is filled; we find the spiritual food needed for doing good works."

"Main Line Protestantism has missed the boat—always dealing with issues on the outside, not the inside."

"I'll second that—especially in places like this suburban community in which we live. It's fatuous to criticize the process, however, because we are doing it here in a place where people work so hard to avoid pain. People will never activate their faith in the world until they can experience their own inner pain and faith."

"You are not able to love Black people in Boston until you love yourself. Your own acceptance of personal imperfection can lead you to an acceptance of others. This is a different understanding of love."

"Of course, a faith empowering session can't do it all. But it does something. There is an opportunity for more follow-through in a meeting with one of the ministers after the actual session. It is wise for one of the ministers to be involved as an extension of pastoral care. If the criticism is too much 'comfort' the last time I presented I was *not* comforted. I was *not* soothed. The passage dealt with David weeping over the death of his son Absalom, and I am trying to let go of my son. Until you can deal with these things you are not free to be in the world in a way that is productive."

"I am now beyond an acquaintance level in my church relationships. I can look across the pews and see a group member and know he (she) is not all right, and then I need to do something."

"It's not just that you go for comfort, although you receive that, but love and compassion which can empower you to live and do. They validate you. I'd offer a word in praise of comfort."

"I have often in the past been frightened off in dealing with an issue. I am on an important board of directors, where I have felt empowered to raise the issue of our investments in South Africa. Perhaps the resolution may be no different, but I have more courage in saying: 'I don't want to vote on this yet.' I can turn back on myself more calmly, and express myself in a way that bears witness to my conviction, even among people more powerful than I could ever think of being. When we talk of racism, we are talking fear and ignorance. I can now push this issue beyond the first rank. I never would have done so before."

"Comfort—is that a negative? I don't think anyone can experience inward growth without its having an impact on their outward lives, their family, their work, everything."

"Doesn't comfort literally mean 'strength with someone else?' Isn't it to move beyond being either macho or guilt-ridden? We have talked of the Holy Spirit, which the Bible calls Comforter—a source of strength. Without qualm, I say I am comforted, and thus reinvigorated to do new things."

"I think there has been a lot of trust here to dare to let something of a house-church (or churches) live on their own, without ministers feeling threatened by not being able to call the direction those house-churches will take. I think what we've said here is that we trust you in your relationship with God. That is the foundation for the ministry of the laity."

* * *

Such is the testimony of the nine five-year faith empowering veterans we gathered one summer evening. There is strong affirmation in the above of that small group experience, hints of personal spiritual growth in group participants, and statements of hope that others might try a process which has contained such meaning for those who have been involved. There are also reminders that every process is imperfect and that no process can accomplish everything.

Before we go on to a more theoretical consideration of the faith developmental foundations and expectations of our work, we would like to comment, briefly, on the two "recurring criticisms" that Bill mentioned above to the nine veterans.

The first of those recurring criticisms was that faith empowering might be a comfortable "parlor game," simply making us feel good as we sit talking in living rooms, without helping to change the world towards greater social justice. We believe that the six-step process does need to be measured constantly against this standard. And we are not convinced that the faith empowering groups in our experience always come out as positively as they could in that measurement. Yet we can affirm that our strategy is close to others which have empowered social change.

There are similarities, for example, between faith empowering groups and the "base communities" which originated in the 1960's in Central and South America, and which have spread around the world. The latter are small house churches where lay people meet to try to relate scripture and life experience. These base communities see themselves as profoundly involved in their participants' political and economic experiences of oppression and in helping these participants to work to overcome that oppression. Base communities have been a major source of liberation theology, a major stream of renewal within the Church of Jesus Christ.

The faith empowering groups in our experience have been less involved in political and economic oppression, and in social justice issues, than Latin American base communities. Part of the reason here undoubtedly is that the experience of political and economic oppression is less present to many affluent suburban Americans than to their Latin American brothers and sisters in faith.

But faith empowering groups have been able to keep an eye on social justice issues, not only the ones we can easily "see" on our own, but also the ones that others may "see" for us but that we, through the blinders of social privilege or status, may try to ignore. Admittedly, no six-step process can guarantee that its users pay attention to social justice issues. The best pressure towards such attention is the diversity of background, experience, and sensitivity of group members. In any case, there is always a need for privileged Christians to be concerned—in thought, prayer and action—with issues of justice, both personal and social. And the faith empowering process can, we believe, contribute towards serving that goal.

Harvey Cox writes of the experience of base communities in Holland. His words provide helpful perspective on the task of biblical interpretation in faith empowering groups as well:

> For these Dutch base communities it is precisely the challenge of their being largely middle class which they hope their study of the Bible will help them see in critical perspective. Hence they insist that the "reconciliation" of which the Bible speaks should not be used to gloss over conflict, that it requires a

conversion on the part of comfortable Christians, a conversion that will enable them to open their lives to the mentally ill, the physically handicapped, the poor and other disprivileged peoples. These groups also emphasize the idea that biblical "salvation" means "an exodus in which all forms of injustice are left behind, as are all relationships whereby people are pressed into service and demeaned."[4]

The second recurring criticism was that the faith empowering process may not be able to handle responsibly all of the high-powered, occasionally deeply threatening, issues of human broken-ness that presenters might bring to it. We can only begin to respond by acknowledging the reality of such a risk. When all is said and done, no human process, we believe, can finally guarantee against being overwhelmed by a potent issue.

And yet we take comfort in the fact that in our experience of over two hundred actual faith empowering group meetings, the six-step process has held up remarkably well to whatever issues or concerns presenters have brought to those sessions. Part of the reason for such a good track record here is our insistence on preparation sessions before faith empowering group meetings. These preparation sessions provide an important opportunity for group enablers to exercise responsible pastoral supervision over the issues to be considered. Enablers can steer presenters away from issues that may be too explosive or too sensitive to be dealt with creatively and into channels that may have more potential for the empowering of faith.

We have also found in our experience that faith empowering groups have occasionally gotten into more difficulties when they have strayed from the carefully structured process of the six steps than when they have followed those steps more carefully. The six steps do have healthy checks and balances built in to them to aid groups in dealing with potentially troublesome issues in productive ways.

Still, there is a possibility that a particularly high-powered or threatening issue might overwhelm a faith empowering group ses-sion—as such an issue might do to any church program. We would urge those who sponsor a faith empowering program, therefore, to stay in close pastoral communication with faith empowering groups and their members. This communication is useful, not only to guard against problems, but also to help affirm the tremendous growth that such a process can bring to group members.

Against the background of this testimony from veteran faith em-powering group members, and against the background of this treat-ment of recurring criticisms of faith empowering groups, let us turn to the faith developmental foundations of our work.

Faith Development

Some years ago, one of us (Joe) claimed some days alone to reflect on the meaning behind the faith empowering method from the vantage point of faith development. I decided to start this time apart with some quiet moments in the cavernous marble chapel of a retreat center. I sat in its cool stillness, listening to its hushed echoes reverberate as though I were in a desolate Grand Central Station. In the quiet, one could hear the distant rumblings of the retired Jesuits who peopled the further corridors.

The chapel was rich in imagery. Stained glass windows high around the dome symbolized life's highest qualities: patience, peace, faith, love, conscience. Yet, what finally compelled me were the two statues on either side of the altar. To the left was the madonna and child—warm, intimate, gentle; to the right a mature Christ—self-composed, serene, alone. And there, as Robert Kegan has seen it, was the life "dance"[5] once again reflected—the human developmental "dance" between our most inescapable human bonds and intimacies and our need for wholeness and composure and independence. To be so held one knows one is eternally held; to be so whole one becomes a wholly unique self. These are:

> the two greatest yearnings in human experience. . . . One of these might be called the yearning to be included, to be a part of, close to, joined with; to be held, admitted, accompanied. The other might be called the yearning to be independent or autonomous, to experience one's own distinctness, the self-chosenness of one's direction, one's individual integrity.[6]

One would like to think our faith empowering groups support the human momentum lived between these poles of distance and fusion! There have been times of holding (even literally) and times of letting go. There have been times when permission has been given, tacitly, for people to be who and where they are, even if that does not mean a style of traditional participation in church life at present.

These polarities once found a very powerful centering place in the gift to me of a word picture, shared during my most recent presentation. I was imagined by one of our group members as embracing myself on my own lap, pieta-like. In that moment I felt held by myself in a way evocative of God's holding love. But I also knew myself as the holder, with my own self-chosen integrity. Having once viewed Michaelangelo's Pieta, I found extra power in that image.

Beyond such groups, however, and their gifts in imagery, can we understand this life and faith "dance" more adequately? Can we understand faith development in any way which does not belittle human complexity or reduce our mystery to theory?

Four months into the first year of the faith empowering project we asked group members to write out their understandings of faith. Almost half started such statements with the phrase: "Faith is the belief that. . . ." Wilfred Cantwell Smith in *Faith and Belief*, argues that faith is not "the belief that," in our contemporary usage, for belief, contrary to its own history, has come to mean only intellectual propositions or assertions. Smith writes:

> There was a time when "I believe" as a ceremonial declaration of faith meant, and was heard as meaning: "Given the reality of God, as a fact of the universe, I hereby proclaim that I align my life accordingly, pledging love and loyalty". A statement about a person's believing has now come to mean, rather, something of this sort: "Given the uncertainty of God, as a fact of modern life, so-and-so reports that the idea of God is part of the furniture of [their] mind".[7]

How horribly have we reduced belief in the modern age to mean that the idea of God is part of the "furniture" of a person's mind!

Some faith empowering group members were rightly skeptical at first that this experience might only be an attempt to rearrange such furniture. In a speech at a ministry of the laity event, however, one member concluded with these words:

> If at the beginning I had a notion that the experience was a means to arrive at a party line or creed, that notion has been dispelled. This has not been an intellectual exercise; although by no means has it been mindless. Rather, an environment has been created where I, at last, can have a sense of the experience of faith.

Herbert Fingarette has subsumed faith and belief into a prior category of "meaning," a concept "from which one may move either into living or theories about living."[8] In our faith empowering, we have sought together to move into life. We have not wanted to be less than, but *we have wanted to be more than, intellectual* in our approach. We believe it has been a profound educational error in the church as a whole to offer people courses in religious content only rather than to help them compose *meaning* out of their own life tasks, loyalties, loves, and commitments in the light of our biblical tradition. How disempowering it has been to feel that the intellectual furniture of belief in our minds is poorly arranged, inadequate, or altogether missing. Yet, for faithful life in the Spirit we must build *meaning* out of what we have, "the power of shaping into one,"[9] as Sharon Parks has noted. Our faith-forming is no less than "the composing of our life meaning." Faith so stated is the basic, generic human task.

A faith empowering group participant was on to this clue in defining faith for her as "an ongoing dynamic process through which one tries to compose meaning or wholeness out of the surrounding chaos."

Have we said it enough? "The locus of faith is persons. It is persons, not propositions . . ."[10] After the first year of faith empowering experience, group members came up with the following composite of their definitions of faith:

Faith is:
—a search for meaning
—a covenant in shared exploration
—an assurance one gets from a placing or putting of belief
—a knowing there is an answer in images
—an acting on our immediate identity
—the way we deal with people
—to risk, trust, comprehend
—a commitment to search for the godliness in life nurtured by our communion with each other.
Faith embraces everything.
Your God, at the center, holds it all together.

Our task in faith as people who live by meaning is to be about our spiritual growth and development. And yet implicit in this primary human task is a secondary one, at least for those who take seriously not only their own religious lives, but the spiritual lives of others. That task is one of sponsoring ways, strategies, experiences, and vehicles through which human faith may develop.

James Fowler has written extensively about faith development. Many more have re-presented his basic theory in such accessible ways that we will not seek to do so in full here. We do wish, however, to underscore our point above that to help another grow in faith one might plan intentional opportunities which support the natural, more or less unintentional, ways that faith itself develops.

The *adult faith journey*, according to Fowler, occurs through three particular stages which seem to move from dependence to independence to interdependence. The idea of stages is, admittedly, a theoretical way of speaking. But there does seem some confirming truth between Fowler's theories and our own awareness of the types of presentations in faith empowering groups. The flow from dependence to independence to interdependence does shape the three master movements of the adult faith symphony, as unique as each person's own narrative and growth may be. And our process has sought to enable growth within this flow without imposing any built-in upper limit of development.

Let us explain.

The first movement. . . . Fowler calls it the "synthetic-conventional" stage of faith.[11] Kegan speaks of the "interpersonal self."[12] A third writer, John Westerhoff, refers here to a *style* of faith which is "affiliative" or accepting of a basic belonging.[13] We will call this first movement "dependence," for simplicity's sake. This is a style of faith which grabs onto the biblical story and the traditions of the faith community, and which defines itself by the conventions of that community. Acceptance is key in this time of conformity with the values and expectations of authorities. One may, and often does, possess deeply held faith convictions, but they have not yet been held up for critical examination. Perhaps the saying of Robert Frost's neighbor in the poem "Mending Wall" is illustrative: "He will not go behind his father's saying, . . . 'Good fences make good neighbors.' "[14]

Kegan speaks of the need to be "embedded in mutuality" with regard to this qualitative time.[15] Faith empowering groups have certainly offered an experience of such deep mutuality. We recall the poignant progress of a brilliant young woman in one of our groups, taking the critical risk of becoming "interpersonal" by sharing for the first time in a group the life story of her strongly deprived and isolated childhood.

Our groups appear to be fertile ground for the faith developmental task of "the forming of a personal myth . . . of one's own becoming in identity and faith."[16] Perhaps we do not know our own personal myth, our own appropriation of the basic life-traditions we each inherit, until we hear ourselves tell it to others!

Faith empowering groups, in the first year or two of existence, have seemed in our experience to concentrate most often on the sharing and appropriation of each other's "master stories," key ingredients of which are shared in presentations. Yet one starts to hear the transition to the second movement of adult faith as those presentations more critically examine authorities, such as parents, mentors, and additional "significant others," as a way of knowing oneself more truly.

The second movement . . . Certainly, James Fowler has not enhanced the popularity of his work by choosing such seemingly obscure names as "individuative—reflective" faith.[17] Decoded, this simply means a faith stance that is more independent, more individualistic and reflective. The tradition is more critically examined; assumptions previously made are now up for challenge, or at least analysis. Kegan refers to this as the time of the "institutional self," which is more self-initiating from the perspective of an ego center in control.[18]

As intimated above, faith empowering presentations on numerous occasions have focused on relationships with parents, whether living or deceased. One senses a profound adult need to come to terms with our most central of all authority relationships—the internalized image we have of our mothers and our fathers. And such coming to terms can mean becoming "more independent, more individualistic and reflective" about these important life figures. . . . A gift of insight came to one woman presenter as she realized that within herself her father held out a disapproval of her professional role, even from "beyond the grave," sometimes undermining her self-confidence. And that insight led her to a greater sense of personal freedom.

Such concerns seem akin to Fowler's opinion that for a "genuine move" into this stage "there must be an interruption of reliance on external sources of authority."[19] What Sharon Parks has called "the tyranny of the *they*" must be undermined. Faith empowering groups have offered opportunities to exorcize, or at least bring to light, such tyrannical ghosts.

We believe the structure of our process is helpful here in absenting the sometimes "tyrannical they" of clergy. Lay participants have commented decisively that one of the most growth-inducing aspects of these groups is the need for the group to rely on its own leadership resources. Clergy have too often tried to be and do everything, with a well-intentioned but disempowering result. For this reason, we clergy chose not to be participants in lay groups for at least the first years of their life together.

Westerhoff refers to a time of "searching faith."[20] And faith empowering groups often ask the probing question, "But what does it all mean for me?" . . . There comes to mind a breakfast preparation session during the first year. A man wanted to explore as his presentation the meaning of Rabbi Kushner's popular book, *When Bad Things Happen to Good People.*[21] We kept trying to get him to personalize his thoughts, but he simply couldn't. It flashed into mind that here was a person in the throes of seeking to understand his faith intellectually, and this need could only be honored or we would soon make him feel rejected and inadequate. Men in particular, it seems, need to wrestle longer with the intellectual challenge of coming into faith. This is exactly the dynamic of Job, the classic biblical figure who sought to understand rationally what it was that God meant and intended.

Fortunately, our groups have been tolerant, supportive, and non-judgmental towards members' deeper searchings and doubtings. We say fortunately, for this is a crucial time of the ego's coming into its own power as the controlling manager or "administrator" of the self. Yet, while the person needs to participate in a "culture of self-authorship,"[22] he or she also needs sources of value and traditional meaning to stay in place as foils for that very development.

One is reminded of D.W. Winnicott's idea of a "holding environment" conducive to growth: "It must hold on. It must let go. And it must stick around so that it can be reintegrated."[23] The "holding on" support at this time in a person's faith development may be paradoxically in giving permission to "let go!" A church, no less than a faith empowering group within it, may be instructed by this dynamic: if a response to a faith-challenge is dogmatic, the challenger may either have to leave the environment in order to keep growing, or give up growth. Such is the dynamic, too, of children who find it more difficult, but still imperative, to leave authoritarian parents if they are to claim their autonomous lives.

An enormous question for the church is posed by Robert Kegan in this regard. Do we permit others "to transcend an ultimate loyalty to the institution-as-it-is?"[24] If we do not, we not only force persons away, but we forfeit a source for transforming the life of the community itself.

Part of us decries the use of such potentially abstract theory. Yet sometimes we discern that the backdrop for a presented issue is a developmental agenda. The aim here is not to reduce persons to stages or theorems, but out of a pastoral heart to understand more compassionately the meaning-making and faith-forming they express.

We hope our process will aid the time for a searching faith. We know it will for those who are patient and willing to move beyond easy answers and simple solutions, such as "the Bible says . . ." or "reason says . . ." To weather the storm of such a searching time is to move on in faith to the third movement. . . .

If the first movement is characterized by dependence and the second by independence, then the third movement of adult faith is the more complex in its theme of interdependence. (Fowler uses the term here, "conjunctive faith,"[25] and Kegan, though not necessarily referring to exactly the same dynamics, speaks of the "interindividual" self.[26]) The now more autonomous ego has grown in relinquishing control needs. Indeed, persons at this time will agree with Jung's general definition of maturity as the ego's relinquishing its necessity for absolute control. With the mid-life voyage comes the possibility for an emergent deeper self—and the listening to deeper voices. Broader aspects of the self speak. Life opens up to a more-than-rational dimension; spirituality flowers. With a mellowing comes a playfulness, a new tolerance for ambiguity.

James Fowler's words regarding his own experience with scripture are important not only for psychological understanding, but for connection with our process. He relates that through an Ignatian method of scriptural interpretation he learned "to relinquish initiative to the text. . . . I began to learn how to let the text *read me.*"[27] This is what often happens when an imaginative process is employed with scripture. One no longer merely interprets scripture but permits scripture to interpret oneself. Paul Ricoeur speaks of a "second naïveté,"[28] which we have mentioned above in chapter seven, as another way of describing a return to the power of symbols and images.

Perhaps those who would question the validity of these movements psychologically could find them descriptive of *educational* approaches, for our faith empowering process corresponds to this "third adult movement" pedagogically. In all honesty, for that reason some persons have not been that comfortable with the process. It feels too playful and non-rational for their comfort. Others who have experienced it over the years, in the main, have moved from occasional disappointments that it did not go where people wanted, expected, or needed, into an expectation that in the serendipitous nature of the group exchange, fresh insight and a more empowered faith will ensue.

A final word about faith development and social justice. We have mentioned above in this chapter the recurring criticism that faith empowering groups might become comfortable living-room discussion groups, divorced from the justice issues that fill the broken world around us. Ronald Marstin confirms the point that faith development does ultimately relate to social justice: ". . . Issues of social justice will emerge as the central problems with which a maturing faith will have to deal. Issues of social justice are essentially about who is to be cared for and who neglected, who is to be included in our community of concern and who excluded, whose point of view is to be taken seriously and whose ignored."[29] Inner transformation is important, he adds, "but, failing action, there is no real change."[30] ". . . Mature faith is of its very nature a faith to celebrate the remaking of the world in justice."[31] Marstin reminds us, then, that because faith empowering groups are concerned about the development of faith, they need to be measured against a standard that includes their ability to stimulate social justice.

Empowering

We are aware that, for lack of a better term, we have used the term "empowering" with impunity and without clarity, even as we *have* given a fairly clear context for how we are using the concept of faith itself. We have intimated that intentional processes and strategies can permit, and even more readily, can facilitate faith to grow. We have implied that such a process may incorporate a greater growth potential the more it contains an open ceiling of growth. But we are *not* making any claim that this methodology in any ascertainable way has "developed" faith, in the sense of inciting someone to move from one "stage" to the next. Such may indeed have been the case from time to time, but we have never attempted to "stage" a person's faith before or after some years of immersion in this process. Such might be fruitful for those of a more clinical inclination, but it has not been our bent.

Even James Fowler states that: "I never tried to argue that the structural 'style' of a person's or community's faith is more determinative for their lives and action than their centering values, their images of power or the master stories they take as descriptive of reality."[32]

We have sought to help people center their values more deeply in the Bible, to draw on that source for its wealth of images, and to connect their life stories with those of a divine master. We believe that faith, however described, is empowered by connecting the pieces of the biblical myth (its underlying pattern of meaning) with our own meaning-making attempts.

And, at just this point the "hermeneutics" (or interpretation theory) of Carl Jung may shed a little light. In speaking of Freud's method of psychoanalysis, Jung described his mentor's approach as one of *reduction*. The oft-cited examples of towers, etc. as phallic symbols come immediately to mind, where an image in the unconscious is analyzed and reduced to its symbolic meaning. Jung proposed in addition to this a method of interpretation known as *ampli-*

fication. In such a method, imagination is used to associate and amplify images, and thus meanings.[33] This is roughly analogous to the way in which we have used biblical interpretation in our process, especially in the steps of image pooling and making connections, as discussed in chapters six and seven.

What, for example, Bultmann suggests in biblical interpretation theory as de-mythologizing (see chapter seven), we see correlated to the reductive method of interpretation in Jung's thinking. As our group members pool images out of their unconscious sources, they are instead *re*-mythologizing their life of faith. It is this more-than-rational process which goes to the heart of *empowerment.*

To amplify images accessible to the believer is to empower that person's faith. This is to move by means of what Jung calls the *directed* thinking of our consciousness into the *imaginal* "thinking" world of the unconscious. Allowing images to come forth from the collective wellsprings of biblical tradition, as well as from our more personal sources, is to revive faith, to freshen the conscious faith by baptism in its source waters.

It is then our assumption, psychologically, theologically, and ped-agogically, that we can complete the circle of interpretation by those methods which move us imaginatively into more than one "horizon of meaning:" scripture and personal life experience, individual and group, conscious and unconscious.

This is how we see some crucial meanings behind our method. Intellectually, we have sought to know how and why we are on the right track because intuitively we have sensed *that* we are on that track. When a leader and presenter have left our offices after a preparation session, and when we have discussed an important life concern and found a way for that concern to be connected with scripture, we sense that we are doing more potently what we are called to do and to be in Christian ministry and community.

For witness, we do not resort to more theory, but to telling stories. One remembers the woman many years ago who sat in Bill's study, the Bible upon her lap open to Romans 8. The leader for the upcoming session was also there. They were all good friends. Her faith was admired; she herself was greatly appreciated in our church family. It was hard for her to say it—we're not sure she had said anything like it before. But she did. She read the words, "We know that in everything God works for good with those who love [God]." (verse 28). And she relayed how she had always accepted and believed those words. But now she was struggling. Out of her deep caring for others she told the story of four tragic deaths that had struck around her in the past years, leaving a wake of desolation. When she had blurted out all of these stories, she cried.

After some exploration of her feelings, the three of them sought an appropriate passage of scripture. Jesus in the Garden of Gethsemane emerged as the choice, with a focus on the words, "Not my will, but thine, be done." (Luke 22:42) Bill then took a risk with her. "You know," he offered, "I'm not sure those words really worked for Jesus." She was all ears, for she in truth had heard them as another patronizing prescription, like: handle with prayer. "Wasn't there a sequence to Christ's words, where first he asked for the cup of suffering to be taken from him—and only then did he try to accede to God's will? Yet, even that acceptance did not take care of it all, for he still cried out from the cross, 'My God, my God, why hast thou forsaken me?' " (Matthew 27:46)

She pondered. She was, not unlike Jesus, being called from faith into faith. Faith with the Christ was not a prescription, but as a companion.

Can bringing such companionship into our own lives do anything less than empower our own faith?

11/Variations on the Theme

The following represent a number of usable variations on a faith empowering theme. The final variation in this chapter, Group Bible Study, and A Plan for an Orientation to Faith Empowering (see chapter twelve) are processes we believe to be of special interest.

A. *Social Justice Implications.* A concern for social justice implications is an attempt to move faith empowering groups out of the living room, where they may be tempted to stay, into the world, where they need to go. Step six of the faith empowering process includes the sharing by any group members who so wish of "whatever personal implications or directions for the future the session may have brought to light." Obviously, such sharing could, and should, include a sharing of the social justice implications of the group session—as well as a sharing of the more individual personal life and faith implications of the session. The Christian life, we believe, has both personal and social dimensions. Yet, a faith empowering group might want to highlight the importance of social justice by asking *openly and specifically* in step six for group members to articulate the social justice implications of that session. In this way, the group could point more explicitly towards the importance of the wider issues of justice in our society which need to be related to a vital and growing Christian faith.

B. *Non-Rotating Leadership.* We believe that one of the major values of the faith empowering process is the opportunity it provides for leadership training and experience through rotating the leadership role within the group. It would be possible, nonetheless, if a group so chose, for one person to serve as permanent group leader. Group dynamics and experience with a permanent leader are obviously different from what happens in a group with rotating leadership. But the option of a permanent leader is one possible variation on a faith empowering theme that could be tried.

C. *After-Session With Presenter and Enabler.* The presenter at a faith empowering group meeting may wish to meet with the enabler after the session to discuss and reflect on what happened in that session. It may be important for the presenter to debrief feelings, expectations, insights, and disappointments. Whereas we have not found such an after-session to be needed for every group meeting, we have found that the offering of such a possibility is important. And occasionally, when people have taken up the offer, such an after-session has proved to be particularly valuable.

D. *Semi-Annual Group Review.* One of the weaknesses of the faith empowering six-step process by itself is that it does not provide time within those six steps for presenters from previous sessions to share with the group how their life has been going since the session of their sharing, and to receive group feedback. We realize, of course, that no finite process can do everything. Nonetheless, because of the limitations of the six-step process itself, we would recommend that a faith empowering group supplement its regular sessions with semi-annual group review sessions. Such supplementary sessions should include an opportunity for each presenter in the past half-year to review with the group whatever they wish to share about the ongoing life of their personal presentation following the session in which they first shared.

E. *Church Business Meeting Technique.* All or part of the faith empowering process can be used as a technique to deal with church business. We have had some experience here, from difficult budget priority decisions, to a decision about some possible changes in the regular Sunday order of worship. Though we do not see faith empowering necessarily as a technique to deal with every issue, we can point to some significant results when it has been tried. In this church business meeting technique, the item to be considered becomes the "personal presentation" of step two. A single "presenter" may share that item, or those members of the group who have input may be invited to contribute their understanding of the issues, including the personal impact they see in those issues. Then, after the issues have been thoroughly laid out, the group leader reads a pre-selected biblical passage that relates to the business item, and someone reads a guided meditation written ahead of time as a preliminary "bridge" between the business item and scripture. (We should note here that the guided meditation should not be written as an attempt to "load" the issues or "solve" the problems!) The group then engages in image pooling and an attempt to make connections between the business item, the scripture passage, and the guided meditation. The closing sharing by the group of the implications of this faith empowering session would then become the group's decision-making on the business item. What can happen with such use of faith empowering techniques is that a group can deal with its issues with greater imagination, depth, and spirit than is often the case in business meetings. (Such a usage is hardly new. An Ignatian method of group discernment has been utilized effectively in Roman Catholic communities for just such decision-making.)

F. *One-Shot, Large Group Sessions.* Occasionally, we have found the need for a faith empowering experience in a large group of people on a one-shot basis (rather than in the context of a long term commitment to a small group). In such a case, we have found it possible to do **steps two and three, four, and six** in the *large group*, and **steps two and five** in spontaneously formed *pairs* and *dyads*. Brief community building and prayer are done in the large group. Then step two, the "personal presentation," is done in pairs, with each partner taking a turn sharing in response to some common, probing question. The group is called back together for the reading of a biblical passage relating to the common question, for the reading of a guided meditation based on that scripture, and for image pooling. Then, in the same pairs, each person tries to make connections, with their partner's help, between their earlier sharing, the scripture, and the guided meditation. Finally, back in the large group, people are invited to share the implications of the session for them. While the fact of the spontaneous step-two sharing in pairs means that the scripture reading and guided meditation may turn out to be more distantly related to the content of that sharing than one might hope, still this one-shot variation on a theme can give a representative taste of the six-step faith empowering process to a relatively large group of people.

G. *Assimilation of New Members.* Churches are rightfully concerned about the need to incorporate new members into the ongoing life of the congregation, once they have joined. One church we know of has considered adopting a faith empowering program as that congregation's basic strategy to assimilate new members.

H. *Clergy Support Group.* The life of an ordained minister can be a stressful and lonely one. One way to deal with both the stress and the loneliness would be to gather a group of clergy—either a denominational or an ecumenical group—for regular faith empowering experiences. We have had some experience with an ecumenical faith empowering support group, and we have found that experience to be both moving and rewarding for those who have participated.

I. *Seminary Field Education Group.* One of the ways in which theological seminaries educate men and women for ministry is through field education in local congregations or other settings. Seminarians engaged in such field education could use the faith empowering process as the basis of a group for support, accountability, and ongoing reflection. Experiences in the field education site could become the personal presentations in step two of the six-step process.

J. *Lay Ministry Support Group.* Many contemporary churches are trying to take more seriously the vocation of all Christians, clergy and laity, to be ministers of Jesus Christ in the church and in the world. We have discovered that the faith empowering process can be of value as a structure for a lay ministry support group. One lay person, for example, decided to share as her personal presentation some of the dreams and frustrations she was experiencing in her work as a social worker. A support group then followed the rest of the steps of the six-step process in the hope of empowering both her faith and her ministry in the world. The occasion proved to be one of deep meaning and value both for the woman and for the group as a whole.

K. *Reflection on Outreach Action.* An important method of learning is the **action-reflection model.** In this model, we act, then we reflect on our action, then we act again in the light of our reflection, then we reflect again, etc. Reflection here is a constant companion to action, helping us to learn from our mistakes, to understand our successes, and to search for the meaning of what we are doing. The faith empowering process can be used for the reflection part of an action-reflection model of learning. A group of people engaged in outreach, for example, might use the six-step process to complement their action.

L. *Preaching and the Merging of Horizons.* The biblical interpretation theory behind the merging of biblical and contemporary horizons (see especially the section on biblical interpretation in chapter seven) can be useful beyond the faith empowering process. Sound preaching could be built on the methodology of merging horizons. A sermon may speak with most power and faithfulness when it is conceived and delivered by one who has found an imaginative way to merge the horizons of scripture with the horizons of contemporary life.

M. *Merging Horizons and Church Programming.* The merging of horizons may serve as a theoretical foundation for the faith empowering process (see especially the section on biblical interpretation in chapter seven) and for preaching (see "L" immediately above). The theory may also be useful in conceiving and planning the total church program. Programs in Christian education, outreach, music, stewardship, drama, art, membership enlistment, liturgy, spirituality, etc., can find important depth and power as they grow out of imaginative efforts to merge the horizons of the Bible and the modern world.

Group Bible Study

Any size group may participate
Come for any one session, or for a series

Total time for Group Bible Study is approximately 90 minutes
(Suggested timing for each step is given in parentheses)

Step 1/Sharing and Prayer. (20 minutes)
This step is the same as the first step in the faith empowering process. The opening sharing should include sharing of names and should relate to the basic themes of the biblical passage about to be considered.

Step 2/Reading of Biblical Passage and Guided Meditation. (15 minutes)
The leader reads a pre-selected (and, if desired, pre-announced) biblical passage, and then the leader invites the group to relax and leads the group in a guided meditation on that passage which she or he has composed prior to the meeting. (It is helpful if the leader has read biblical commentaries before composing the guided meditation.)

Step 3/Personal Reflection and Sharing. (15 minutes)
The group is asked to reflect in silence on the biblical passage and guided meditation, seeking points of contact between that passage and meditation and their own personal experience. Journal writing is welcome if you wish. At the end of a period of silent personal reflection, group members will be invited to share whatever they wish—in pairs or triads or in the whole group—from the personal experiences on which they have been reflecting.

Step 4/Re-Reading of Biblical Passage and Image-Pooling. (15 minutes)
The leader will re-read the biblical passage from step two. The group as a whole will then be invited to pool whatever images come out of that passage (on newsprint), understanding that these images will be informed by the guided meditation and personal reflection/sharing, but focusing the image-pooling on contemporary meanings of the biblical passage.

Step 5/Making Connections—Merging Horizons. (10 minutes)
The whole group will seek to make connections between the contemporary meanings of the biblical passage and our total experience as a church in the modern world.

Step 6/Sharing Implications and Closing Prayer. (15 minutes)
The leader will invite any group members who so wish to share the implications of the meeting for them: "What implications does the biblical passage in question have for us personally, for our shared communal life, or for our life in the world?" The leader will then lead the group in a closing and summary prayer.

12/How to Get Started

Afew years ago we gathered together, for the first time, the persons who ended up being the "pioneers" of this faith empowering process. They came together in a retreat intended to introduce them to a process which was at that stage only an untested design. We were wise, we think, to give persons with exploratory interest an opportunity to learn about faith empowering, and to taste it a bit, before asking them to make any commitment. The forty or so persons who did eventually make the leap of faith with us at the end of the retreat were more trusting because of that shared experience, and willing on the basis of a fairly in-depth initial exposure to give the process a try. We think people interested in promoting faith empowering groups in other settings would be wise to use the same or a similar approach.

But before we go on to share in more detail some resources in that regard, we affirm that certain steps prior to a "public offering" are equally important, if not more so, whether the process is being promoted through a local church, a theological seminary, a denominational judicatory, or some other group. Two steps are absolutely indispensable: the first is to obtain official sponsorship in the initiating organization, and the second is to find a qualified "advisor" for the process.

The Role of a Sponsoring Group in Launching Faith Empowering

Those with a few years of experience in the life of the church or any other institution will recognize the strategic importance of enlisting the support and sponsorship of an appropriate group within that institution, which will help to legitimate and promote any new program offering. In a local church this would most appropriately be a Board of Deacons, Elders, or Christian Education; a Vestry; a professional staff, or other. Some churches have specialized Adult Education Committees. In a theological seminary or other academic institution there may well be a Spiritual Life Committee or some similar group. Denominations at their various levels of bureaucracy, no doubt, have committees or groups whose sponsorship and support could be sought.

The overriding concern here is the well known issue of ownership. One can often find one or two other persons of keen interest who will help to carry forward the initial stages of the project, and who might be led to participate in an ongoing way. It is also more convincing to publicize such a new opportunity with the backing of a group which has recognized credibility and authority. And starting a new venture within a group is always a more fulfilling way to proceed for those wanting to take leadership in such a venture.

Such a sponsoring committee which has an ongoing life in the institution can also help to keep the process "on track" from year to year, should it catch on. Faith empowering groups typically covenant for one year together, and someone needs to promote groups afresh in subsequent years, and offer some ongoing monitoring.

While we have not had any negative experiences here, such a sponsoring committee could also intercept in a responsible way any problems as they arise. We recall hearing of a church that developed some very complicated negative dynamics after using a house church model of several small groups, which some members joined and others did not. This resulted in a divided church. A sponsoring committee would take responsibility for the creative interface between this offering and the ongoing healthy life of the broader institution.

Sponsorship can also help in accomplishing other logistical tasks such as publicity, organizing meeting details, refreshments, etc. Some funding may also be indicated, although one of the beautiful things about faith empowering groups in our church is that in six years, we have not budgeted one penny!

The Qualities and Role of an Advisor

The second, but absolutely indispensable, step in developing faith empowering groups is establishing the best person available in the role of advisor, or what we like to call an "enabler" to the process. Given biblical training, professional staff members may be the best to serve in such a capacity, but not necessarily! While faith empowering could foreseeably be started without a sponsoring committee, the process would founder without the creative leadership of an enabler. We would like, then, to surface what we think the qualities and role of the advisor should be.

When we speak of *qualities*, here, we are referring first and foremost to a spiritual giftedness. The advisor needs to be a person of faith and creative imagination who can connect with people meaningfully and trustingly. In addition, the person needs to have sufficient experience with the Bible to be able to draw upon its contents imaginatively and intuitively. Academic training in the Bible at the seminary level is clearly not a prerequisite. While it might be helpful, the faith empowering process utilizes, as we hope you have noted, a method of interpretation which is not primarily intellectual. Neither is it anti-intellectual, we hasten to add. But our point is that a person with years of devotional use of the Bible, and who, with or without formal degrees, knows this book as a source of meditation and inspiration, may well be the person you want to enlist as your advisor. It is possible, too, that certain clergy with a very rationalistic and exclusively intellectual approach to scripture would not have the qualities for successful leadership with this process. In general, you should look for a person of transparent faith, capable of relating effectively to others, who has a good connection with the biblical story and its relevance.

The *role* of the enabler is simpler to assert. Certainly this person should be found before the process is initiated, as the credibility of this person's leadership will be equated with the potential in the process. An initial part of the role, then, is to help to launch the group through an opening retreat or workshop offering (see example which follows). The ongoing role is to meet monthly as facilitator of the preparation meetings before each faith empowering session.

An enabler needs also to be willing to give some ongoing support to the leaders, who may need further consultation about any part of the process, including the opening prayer and the prayer for the last step. He or she might also profit by some suggestions for the guided meditation. Here we could point to the material in chapter five of this book which could be used as handouts. We could also suggest commentaries or other interpretive materials which provide resources and background for the biblical passage. We may note in this connection that the Bible commentaries on the shelves of our church library have circulated more actively as leaders explored background for their guided meditations.

During the preparation session, the advisor might also express a willingness to meet with the presenter following the faith empowering session itself. Sometimes such a post-meeting can help consolidate gains by offering an additional opportunity for reflection or debriefing.

The final ingredient in the enabler's "job description" is to offer some "whole group meetings," especially throughout the first year in which faith empowering groups meet. We found it helpful to begin with some orientation opportunity like the one which follows to expose people who have exploratory interest to the process. After persons have committed to participate, they will be helped if other meetings are arranged in addition to the faith empowering sessions themselves. You could arrange this in short meetings which cover only one topic, or in a longer workshop format. It would be important to cover such topics as "active listening" and other communication skills-training appropriate to the non-advice-giving, non-problem-solving approach used in faith empowering. It would also be important to review examples of presentations, to practice guided meditation writing, and to go over what is involved in effective leadership in the six-step process.

A Plan for an Orientation to Faith Empowering

The following is a brief sketch of one possible plan for orienting new people to the faith empowering process. The sketch is a design for an overnight retreat, beginning with supper on Friday night and lasting till late afternoon on Saturday. (You are obviously free to modify the design and the time period to fit your particular hopes and needs.)

Friday evening of a faith empowering orientation retreat could consist of an introduction to steps one, two, and three of the six-step process, gradually building on, and reinforcing, learnings as people proceed.

Step One

- The retreat leader leads the whole group in a pre-selected community building exercise. For example, the group might be invited to express their current mood through a weather image, or they might be invited to describe a role they play in the life of the church through an image of a part of an automobile. (Review chapter three to stimulate your own creativity.)

- The whole group is then asked to brainstorm other ideas for possible community building exercises which might be used to draw a group together and to help it start to think imaginatively.
- The leader, in prayer, sums up the mood and spirit of the group in its community building so far, and asks for God's presence with the retreat and with its participants.

Step Two

- The retreat leader gives input on the meaning of the term "horizon"—both its technical and its everyday sense. The leader may wish to engage the group in a discussion whose goal is to illustrate our contemporary "horizon." This can be done as simply as pointing to different people in the room and asking them to describe the horizon of what they can see without turning their heads.
- The leader gives input on guidelines for faith empowering personal presentations, based on the guidelines in chapter four. You may wish to pass out copies of those guidelines.
- The leader invites the participants to divide up into small groups (of twos or threes) and to take turns sharing—with the other person or persons doing active listening—a piece of their own personal experience they would like reflected on in the context of faith and the context of a supportive group. The group could be encouraged to try to identify elements of the "horizon" of the pieces of personal experience that are shared.

The group may wish to take a break here.

Step Three

- The retreat leader gives input on the relationship of imagination to discontinuity (the phenomenon that our imagination continues to work on a problem or issue when we *pause* from concentrated attention on that issue to do, or think about, something else; see chapter five). He or she might want to elicit from the group examples of a time when a pause has been creative as a prelude to insight or resolution.
- The leader gives input on guidelines for the choice of scripture

passages which are relevant for faith empowering (see chapter five).

- In the small groups from step two above, participants reflect together on possible scripture passages which might be appropriate for the personal presentations they have just shared with each other.
- The small groups may also want to reflect back on community building exercises which would have been helpful in preparing the way both for the personal presentations they shared, and now for the scripture passages they have selected as appropriate for those presentations.

The retreat leader should then gather the whole group back together and ask for a volunteer to be the presenter in an actual demonstration faith empowering session on Saturday afternoon. The leader would plan to meet with that presenter after the group adjourns for that evening to plan the Saturday afternoon faith empowering session. The leader might well close the evening at this point with worship.

On Saturday morning, the whole group would reconvene to continue working its way through an orientation to the practice and theory of the six-step faith empowering process. As the group gathers, the retreat leader could lead an opening worship experience, including leading the whole group through a pre-written guided meditation as a part of that worship.

Step Three—continued

- The retreat leader would give input on guidelines for writing faith empowering guided meditations (see chapter five).
- The leader may then want to invite the participants to try their own hand at composing a guided meditation on whatever issue or passage of scripture they might choose. If time or your sense of the group's readiness does not permit the actual writing of a guided meditation, small groups could discuss various imaginative approaches to specified parables which might feed in at some point to a guided meditation.

Step Four

- The retreat leader gives more input on imagination, as background theory and context for what is involved in the pooling of images (see chapter six).

• The leader invites one or more volunteers to read out loud the guided meditations they have just written, asking the whole group to listen, and then to pool the images which come to mind from those meditations. If meditations were not actually written, the ideas for imaginative approaches elicited in step three above would be shared at this time.

The group may wish to take a break here.

Step Five

• The retreat leader gives input on the nature of step five of the six-step process: "making connections—merging horizons." Special attention should be given to such issues as the following: the faith empowering session leader needs to serve here as process watchdog; the presenter needs to be the focus of the group discussion; and the faith concerns of the presenter need to become the particular group focus.
• The retreat leader gives input on the nature of the biblical interpretation theory involved in faith empowering (see chapter seven).
• The leader gives a brief review of steps one to five of the faith empowering process.

Step Six

• The retreat leader asks the group to share the implications people have felt and experienced from the retreat so far.
• The leader closes the morning retreat session with prayer.

After lunch, the retreat leader would invite a group of six or seven volunteers to join that leader and to join the person who volunteered late Friday evening to be a presenter. The eight or nine persons total, thus assembled, would engage in an actual faith empowering session, with the retreat leader serving as the leader of that session. The eight or nine would sit in the center of the whole group and "fishbowl" the faith empowering session, allowing retreat participants on the outside circle to listen and observe, but not to participate vocally in the actual faith empowering process.

When the "fishbowl" group has completed the six-step process, those eight or nine persons would move back and rejoin the larger group circle. Participants who have been listening and observing so far that afternoon would then have a chance to share the meaning of the just-completed faith empowering session for them.

Then the afternoon would be open for general questions and discussion, and the retreat may close with worship.

Before participants disperse, it would be wise to hand out an evaluation sheet, which would include an opportunity to express interest in joining a faith empowering group. These forms could be returned at a later date if that is more comfortable. The forms should have a place to check whether definitely interested, not interested, or undecided about future participation in an actual group. One might also wish to have them indicate one or two persons attending the retreat whom they would feel best about having in their faith empowering group, and, with an assurance of confidentiality, persons whom they would not feel comfortable having in their group.

The leader might also inform participants that when the groups have been tentatively configured, participants will receive a confidential phone call for approval before the groups are publicly announced.

Finally, it would be wise to seek commitment and choose a date for a subsequent meeting of all participants, when they would organize their own meeting schedule, choose leaders and presenters for each faith empowering group, and establish the dates of the first preparation meetings. Such a Whole Group Meeting, as we have called them, would quite beneficially include a brush-up review of the process and some skill-training exercises for sensitive interpersonal communications.

Conclusion

A final thought here is the need for courage! This process has become one important tool for adults to enhance their faith understanding. If we were able to start faith empowering groups with only scattered resources for guidance, we feel that others, drawing upon the focused presentation of our work should be heartened to risk replicating our experiment in other ways and places. As we have shared part of our story with you, we are eager to hear stories of ways in which the process developed in one locale unfolds elsewhere.

13/Praying the Word

When we began the faith empowering project, we did not sufficiently understand how empowering it can be, not only to be a presenter in a group session, but also to be the leader. Many persons, some of whose creativity follows, engaged scripture as never before when their turn came to lead the faith empowering process. They have wrestled with us time and again to choose appropriate scripture for the personal presentations. These leaders have then read the passages over and over, read commentaries, jotted down ideas, and finally let their creativity express itself.

Those who are presenters at the faith empowering sessions know what the scripture selection is ahead of time, for they have helped to choose it. But they do not see or read the meditation the leader has prepared. Its creation is a labor of love. It comes to them freshly as a special gift.

Scripture is the key ingredient in the process, transforming group meetings beyond mere psychological sharings into the possibility of faith happenings. The meditations are offered as prayer-like forms, and must be verbalized prayerfully, meditatively.

Perhaps one day we could put together an entire book of guided meditations, in the way we put together cookbooks in the church. We do, indeed, have many more in our files, but share these which follow because they show a range of possibilities. Enjoy our gifts to you. We are indebted to their several authors for willingness to share their creations.

* * *

Guided meditations are best begun with some relaxation instructions. Some of the sample guided meditations which follow include specific instructions to direct listeners into a more receptive mode. Other samples merely indicate that relaxation techniques should be used. A generic example of an opening relaxation approach which could be used with any guided meditation would be the following:

"Relax . . . put yourself into a comfortable position . . . feet lightly on the floor, arms at rest. Take a few moments to be in touch with your breathing . . . your breathing in . . . and your breathing out. . . . Close your eyes.

"Relax your head and neck . . . gently turning your head back and forth, releasing the tension there. Relax your arms, letting the day's tensions flow down from your head. Let them pass down your relaxed arm muscles and out your fingertips.

"Now relax your chest and relax your stomach, waiting for any knots to dissolve. Relax your buttocks . . . your thighs . . . and calves. Let all remaining tensions flow down your body, your legs, and right out your toes.

"Remain in the state of receptive quiet as you listen and enter into the following guided meditation: . . .

Guided Meditation on Genesis 4:1–16

"Cain said to Abel his brother, 'Let us go out to the field.' And when they were in the field, Cain rose up against his brother Abel, and killed him." (Genesis 4:8)

[Relaxation exercises were given at the beginning.]

You, Cain, are in the field, resting at noontime, eating your simple lunch. . . alone. . . stewing. . . .

"Blast that brother of mine! I have had *just about enough* of that Abel! He has been a pain in the neck ever since he was born, and well do I remember *that* day! All of a sudden there was that little red-faced, squalling creature demanding my parents' every attention. What about *me* and *my* needs? . . .

"I can hear my parents now, year after year:" 'You can do it yourself, Cain. You are old enough. Why don't you just *try?* . . . I'm *busy* now, Cain. . . . *Later,* Cain. . . . Leave your brother *alone,* Cain. . . . Why do you get so *angry,* Cain? . . .'

"They have never *understood* me. They have never *listened* to me. *Nothing* I do is satisfactory to them. There is always that (with sarcasm) *perfect* Abel, apple of their eye—or should I say blasted little sheep. That no-good lazy shepherd, lying around in the fields *supposedly* watching those *stupid* sheep while *I* break my back in *real* labor in the fields. What thanks do *I* get?

"I am *sick* and *tired* of the way Abel makes me feel, all this anger and . . . yes, I have to admit it, . . . jealousy. Something has got to change, and it is *not* me. One of these days, he is going to find himself slaughtered, just like one of his sacrificial lambs. Good riddance and peace for me. . . .

"That's a thought! . . . It could look like an accident. When we take our offerings . . . if I am careful no one will suspect murder. He would be out of my life forever. My parents and . . . (uncertainly) yes, . . . even the Lord . . . would see *me,* Cain, and not only me in comparison with Abel. . . . (Excitedly) . . . . Yes, that is the solution, so easy! . . . (Angrily) . . . . Why did I not do it *long* ago? . . . Tomorrow, when we take our sacrifices. . . . Hopefully, no one will be there. . . . (Excitedly) . . . . No one will suspect. . . . Everything will work out just fine. Good riddance, Abel! . . ."

What feelings and images does this drama bring to the surface in you? . . .

Guided Meditation on Genesis 12:1–3 and Hebrews 11:8–10

"By faith Abraham obeyed when he was called to go out to a place which he was to receive as an inheritance; and he went out, not knowing where he was to go." (Hebrews 11:8)

[Get the group to relax. . . .]

The river is far below—blue and green water rushing along its course. The banks are crowded with trees clinging precariously to the steep sides; here and there one leans far over as if to take a refreshing sip of the clean, clear water. We stand at the lookout above, waiting and watching, filled with anticipation. . . . An adventure awaits us. It all began on a glorious summer day at camp way up in the

Northern woods. Cool, fresh air, the sky as blue as turquoise, cloud pictures reflected in the lake below, the scent of pine trees and smoke.

You find yourself hurrying down a winding trail, carrying your tote with a change of clothes. As you turn the last corner, you see that the bus is already there—a big old khaki-colored school bus—and several people are gathered beside it. You approach the group, all strangers, and soon there are introductions and greetings all around. A car pulls up. It is our guide, young, bearded, and looking as if he spends his life out-of-doors. A count is made—yes, we are all there— seven of us. We climb aboard the bus and settle down for the trip. We find ourselves riding through the forests, undeveloped and beautiful. We are traveling on a logging road. Except for a truck now and then, laden with huge logs, we seem to be the only people around. Suddenly we see a huge and magnificent moose in a meadow beside the road.

The other members of the group seem to be full of good spirits and excitement. We are gradually getting acquainted and the initial strangeness is disappearing.

The guide asks for our attention and goes over the plans for the day. He assures us that it will be a trip to remember. Suddenly you find yourself asking silently, "What on earth am I doing here? Why did I decide to come? Will it make any difference if I change my mind? Who needs a white water raft trip anyway?"

Our guide continues with his instructions, showing us how to put on our helmets, our life jackets, and how to use our paddles. Finally he passes out release forms for us to sign. You read them carefully and realize that if you continue, it is because you are willing to accept the challenge and the risk. Our guide is so calm and confident and patient that you find yourself reassured. After all, hundreds of people do this every summer. It's supposed to be fun!

All too soon we are at our beginning point. The raft and gear are unloaded and we stop briefly at the lookout. It will soon be time for the surging water to be released. The river below is filled with rafts loaded with people ready for the trip. There are even some people alone in kayaks.

It is time to carry our things down and take our place on the water. It is the last chance you have to change your mind. You can't believe you're really doing this. You are sure you would rather be back at camp quietly reading a book or taking a nap. What if you are unable to do your share? Will you endanger the others if you don't perform? Do you want to take this risk?

The raft is in the water. The guide is telling us where to sit. You are comforted by the fact that he places you right beside him. You perch on the top of the huge orange rubber tube around the outside. Your foot is securely wedged under the rope, your helmet is fastened, and you are clutching your paddle firmly. We are on the river, we are practicing our strokes, we all listen attentively to every word John says. What's this? We're going around in circles. . . . We learn to take deeper strokes, to balance the forward movement. It is beautiful on the river. . . . The sun is shining. . . . It seems so peaceful.

Suddenly we begin to move—no to *rush* downstream as the pent-up waters are released. . . . We are literally racing along. No time to watch the scenery, we are all paddling and paddling as hard as we can. "White water ahead! Keep it straight, keep it straight!" We have passed the first test. . . . Wet, excited, we can smile at one another. . . . But no time to relax, for we have other challenges to face.

Suddenly, the raft bends in the middle—first the front goes down, then up, sending a huge wave. It hits you and you find yourself knocked to the bottom of the raft. You are in water up to your waist and your foot is under the rubber crossbar. For the first time you feel secure. How nice it would be just to stay there. . . . The sun is warm and the water not too cold and the high sides of the raft protect you, but you can't reach over the side to paddle. Your guide warns you that you are not secure and safe there but in danger, for hidden rocks could be disastrous. Wearily and warily you pull yourself back to the top of the tube. The roar of the water increases, and you know that you are swiftly approaching the greatest challenge of all.

The guide shouts, "When I yell 'stroke' give it all you've got!" What *have* we been doing? You've been giving your all and more since we started! Your arms are aching and your knuckles are white from hanging on to the paddle. And then . . . it is over. . . . We are through the rapids. . . . The roaring of the water diminishes. . . . The angry rushing waves become gentle ripples. We breathe more slowly and evenly. . . . The stress and anxiety are gone. . . . Calm, peaceful waters lie ahead. . . . It is a time for celebration!

When you are ready, share the images, if you will, which come to your mind. . . .

Guided Meditation on Exodus 1:15–21

"Then the king of Egypt said to the Hebrew midwives, one of whom was named Shiphrah and the other Puah, 'When you serve as midwife to the Hebrew women, and see them upon the birthstool, if it is a son, you shall kill him; but if it is a daughter, she shall live.' " (Exodus 1:15–16)

Let's close our eyes—sit quietly—relax—stretch out—take a deep breath . . . let it out . . . and another one. . . .

We are going back to the time of Jacob and his followers, long after they arrived in Egypt, long after the struggle to survive and set down roots in a foreign land. Years and years went by, and the children of Jacob—and then Joseph—*did* survive and grow strong, multiply and prosper. However, along with their good fortune there developed an uneasy feeling in the land. The Egyptians began to view the flourishing Hebrews as a threat, and the new king became alarmed and feared for the future of his people.

To try to break their spirit, Pharaoh saw to it that the Hebrews were made to labor in the heat of the fields, to carry the burden of moving heavy stones to build the cities of the time, to be treated almost as slaves. But the more they were oppressed, the more they thrived! Something more must be done!

You and your friend are Hebrew women. You are midwives. You have been unable to have children of your own and therefore devote yourselves to helping with the deliveries of other women's babies. You feel sad about this in some ways, but happy to be an important part of the joyful arrival of new life into your community.

Suddenly one day, Pharaoh summons you and your friend to his palace. "From now on, when you as midwives attend to the childbirth of the Hebrew women, you must *kill all the male babies!* . . . As for the female babies, they may live," he announced.

You are stunned! Hardly able to keep control, you and your friend manage to bow to Pharaoh and hurry off to find a quiet place to yourselves. Once alone you burst into tears, holding each other desperately, your hearts pounding, your stomachs turning over and over. . . . "What can we do?" you wail. "How can we possibly kill little babies, much less those of our own people?" your friend cries. . . . The thought of Pharaoh comes to you again . . . and the risk, the terrible consequences of not obeying him! Helplessness and fear overcome you again and again. . . . A whirlpool of terror engulfs you both. . . . "God, what will we do?" you both call out. "You *know* we cannot obey the Pharaoh! *Who* can we talk to but *you?* You who have always helped our people, . . . please help us now. . . . Help us to find a way. . . . Help us to be strong, to be calm, to think. . . . *Dear God, help us!*"

You both drag yourselves home carrying the heavy burden of your shared secret. The days go by and you see each other often, you pray together and alone, . . . and you finally form a plan!

Weeks later the Pharaoh becomes aware that male babies are being born to the Hebrew women—as always! You and your friend are again summoned to his presence. "You have let the male Hebrew children live! Why have you done this?" he demands. "Pharaoh," you say timidly, "the Hebrew women are not refined like the Egyptian women, as you know. They are more like animals and are very hardy and independent. They deliver their babies before anyone can get to them!" . . . You wait fearfully for his response, but . . . there is none! You are told to leave immediately. You can hardly contain yourselves as you rush away. . . . Can the plan have worked? . . . The tears of joy run down your faces as you run back to your people. All the days of anguish and despair! Can they be over for now? . . . Can you finally breathe a sigh of relief? . . .

Hold onto this story and think about how you have felt throughout its telling. Perhaps there are images that come to mind? . . . Feelings that touched you? . . .

Guided Meditation on Matthew 1:18–25

"This is the story of the birth of the Messiah. Mary his mother was betrothed to Joseph; before their marriage she found that she was with child by the Holy Spirit. Being a man of principle, and at the same time wanting to save her from exposure, Joseph desired to have the marriage contract set aside quietly." (Matthew 1:18–19; *The New English Bible*)[1]

[Relax.]

Then, as now, it is a time of births. In births, the ordinary is extraordinary, and the extraordinary, ordinary . . . the human and the divine intertwine in the business of birthing. Now, as then, it is a time of births.

But brother Joseph was not ready for a birth, nor was sister Mary . . . but the Holy Spirit is always ready for births . . . and God had waited through a long and painful history to bring this birth into being . . . God's time . . . God's way . . . God's birthing. And Mary, on the receiving end, was pregnant before her marriage to Joseph, pregnant with the Holy Spirit and with God's agenda.

But Joseph was a man of principle. He had made his plans, ordered his chaos, charted his course. He had a sense of direction, and appreciation for timeliness. He knew what he was about, and was skilled at getting from A to B to C. Joseph was respected . . . his reputation was solid. . . . And Mary, Mary would come along. She would mold to his rhythms and move to his drum beat. . . . He loved her . . . more than any other person in the world.

But Joseph, Joseph was a man of principle; and Mary, Mary was pregnant, pregnant by someone other than him, in a season not of his choosing. . . . Run, Joseph, run . . . run from the unusual, run from chaos, run before your reputation is soiled, run lest you lose control, run before your mind springs open. . . . Oh no, Joseph is not a runner . . . except in his mind. Joseph stands—and in his standing, he is consumed by anger and by questions: "Why, why did it not go my way? What have I done and what has been done to me? Who diverted the plan? Who sabotaged my control and rendered me impotent? . . . Who is knocking Mary around, and why is it happening to her and to me? . . . This was my drama and . . . now it is not. What happened to my lead role? . . . My direction? . . . What is left for me except to withdraw from the stage, to relinquish the contract? . . .

A decision made . . . rehearsed . . . re-examined . . . round and round. Sleep comes hard for men of minds, when the As and Bs and Cs are all mixed up . . . when there is too much rubble to sort through . . . when standing bare and wondering 'who am I?' . . . when an outcast to others—and one's self. Sleep comes hard to sensitive, pained men of minds.

But finally, Joseph, the man of principle, is granted the gracious gift of sleep. For some, sleep is the beginning of salvation. . . . Rest your mind, Joseph . . . open your heart. . . . And through Joseph's night of sleep, God penetrates deeply—through the muck, through his baggage, beneath the questions and the anger. . . . Listen to the message . . . "That which is conceived in Mary is of the Holy Spirit!" . . . . God is in control. . . . God is doing this thing. . . . Be neither afraid nor anxious, Joseph . . . only one thing is required of you . . . only one . . . that you name the salvation which is about to be born. . . . When the birth is accomplished, Joseph, name it, first for yourself—and then for all others.

And Joseph woke up and went home to await the birth of the Holy Spirit, and Joseph named the child Jesus . . . Savior.

Now, as then, it is a time of births. . . . What is waiting to be born in you? . . . Can you name it, first for yourself—and then for all

others? . . God and humanity are in the business of birthing . . .
together. Listen to what the Holy Spirit is conceiving in you . . . then
. . . now . . . births. . . .
[Pool images when you are ready.]

First Guided Meditation on Matthew 14:22–33

"Then he [Jesus] made the disciples get into the boat and go before
him to the other side, while he dismissed the crowds. And after he
had dismissed the crowds, he went up into the hills by himself to
pray. When evening came, he was there alone, but the boat by this
time was many furlongs distant from the land, beaten by the waves;
for the wind was against them. And in the fourth watch of the night
he came to them, walking on the sea. But when the disciples saw him
walking on the sea, they were terrified, saying, 'It is a ghost!' And
they cried out for fear. But immediately he spoke to them, saying,
'Take heart, it is I; have no fear.' And Peter answered him, 'Lord, if it
is you, bid me come to you on the water.'" (Matthew 14:22–28).

Now try to relax, close your eyes, and get in a comfortable position. . . .
You are one of the disciples and Jesus has just ordered you to get
into the boat with the others and cross to the other side of the lake.
You see him dispersing the crowd that has just been fed so miracu-
lously.
Imagine evening to be approaching and the light fading. As you
watch Jesus, you sense that his strength is faltering and he again needs
a time and place to be alone with God. The hill that lies before him
symbolizes the strength which he is lacking, and as he climbs it,
looking toward the starlit sky, he begins to be at peace again. He is
alone and at rest while he speaks to God, and is prepared to wait
patiently until God responds to him. When the reply comes, his
period of rest is over and he is ready to return to the lakeside with
renewed strength and power. By being alone with God he could
disengage his thoughts from worldly things. . . .
Meanwhile, you and the other disciples have rowed out to the
middle of the lake. Suddenly a storm comes and buffets your little
boat. You are terrified and feel out of control. You realize that you
need help from beyond yourselves. Even though you have faith, it is
not strong enough to carry you through the storm. Unexpectedly,
when hope is almost gone, you see Christ coming toward you.

Peter is next to you in the boat. When he sees Jesus walking on the water Peter asks the Christ to call to him. Peter then starts off with great confidence, thinking he can do it alone without Christ's help. You wonder if his courage is mixed with cowardice . . . whether he thinks he is stronger then he is. You watch his confidence and pride turn to terror in the face of the storm, until he becomes utterly helpless. Peter finally cries out in terror . . . and . . . Jesus comes to him. . . .

Soon they are both back in the boat, one dry, the other dripping wet. You find yourself mulling over the experience with each pull upon the oar. When you have finally reached the other shore with Peter and Jesus, your feelings begin to form into images.

When you have had time to reflect on this experience of Peter and the other disciples, and on the way in which Jesus himself sought help from God, share your feelings with the rest of the group. . . .

Second Guided Meditation on Matthew 14:22–33

"Then he [Jesus] made the disciples get into the boat and go before him to the other side, while he dismissed the crowds. And after he had dismissed the crowds, he went up into the hills by himself to pray. When evening came, he was there alone, but the boat by this time was many furlongs distant from the land, beaten by the waves; for the wind was against them. And in the fourth watch of the night he came to them, walking on the sea. But when the disciples saw him walking on the sea, they were terrified, saying 'It is a ghost!' And they cried out for fear. But immediately he spoke to them, saying, 'Take heart, it is I; have no fear.' And Peter answered him, 'Lord, if it is you, bid me come to you on the water.' " (Matthew 14:22–28).

Let us sit back and relax. Try to forget the reality of today. Shake your arms; rotate your shoulders; close your eyes; allow your cares to drain away. . . .

Imagine, if you will, that you are a fisher by trade. Your boat is new, strong, well built, able to take a lot of punishment from nature, and equipped with the latest communications equipment and sonar gear to help detect the schools of fish on which your livelihood depends. Fishing for a living today is hard, much as it was in biblical days when Peter and the other disciples worked at it. Tonight the weather forecast calls for cloudy conditions, with cold rain and harsh wind, along with high seas. These are the result of a storm system which is coming up the coast, but which is to veer out farther to sea before reaching the local area. Our intended fishing area should be stormy but not as bad as it would be to the east. Fishing will not be fun at all tonight. In fact, it will be downright mean and unpleasant.

Your two crew members arrive a half-hour before planned departure, and the three of you work to make sure that everything is in readiness, and that everything works. You stow or tie down all loose items so that they will not be hurled around when the boat pitches, rocks, and twists in the bad weather that is expected. The tide is high, and the group of boats that comprise the local fleet start their engines and, one by one, slip out of the protected harbor and into the open ocean. Each skipper has his (her) own ideas as to where the fish are, and the boats soon are out of sight. The schools of fish are hard to find tonight, and the hold is filling up very slowly.

Finally, you locate a large school of the fish that you most want to catch—the ones that will bring the best prices back at the market. Just as you begin to make inroads into filling the fish bins, the radio crackles to life, announcing that the storm is not going to veer away from the coast, as had been predicted earlier, but instead will pass much closer to the local area. This means that the weather will soon turn even meaner—sufficient to test the nerve, the daring, the skill, and also the faith of all aboard. You can hear some of the other boats calling to their base stations that they are going to turn around and head for home. You ponder just what to do. Your boat is strong enough to weather the storm; you feel that you can handle it, since you have been through heavy storms before. Two hours or so extra fishing would fill your hold and make it a good trip. The extra money would mean a better break for your crew. . . . On the other hand, boats have been lost in bad weather such as this.

What should your choice be? To have faith in your boat, and in your own abilities to master whatever problems the storm might throw your way; and faith in the Lord to bring you through it safely? Or should you follow the conservative, probably more prudent, course and quit fishing immediately to head for the shelter of your home port?

What are your reactions to the situation? . . . What are the similarities and differences between the biblical story we read of Jesus and Peter walking on the water in the storm, and this modern setting? . . . What are the images that come to mind from this guided meditation and the personal presentation we have just heard? . . .

Third Guided Meditation on Matthew 14:22–23

"Then he [Jesus] made the disciples get into the boat and go before him to the other side, while he dismissed the crowds. And after he had dismissed the crowds, he went up into the hills by himself to pray. When evening came, he was there alone, but the boat by this time was many furlongs distant from the land, beaten by the waves; for the wind was against them. And in the fourth watch of the night he came to them, walking on the sea. But when the disciples saw him walking on the sea, they were terrified, saying, 'It is a ghost!' And they cried out for fear. But immediately he spoke to them, saying, 'Take heart, it is I; have no fear.' And Peter answered him, 'Lord, if it is you, bid me come to you on the water.'" (Matthew 14:22–28).

[Relax. . . .]

Alice, in *Alice in Wonderland*, meets the Cheshire cat.

"Cheshire-Puss," said Alice, "would you tell me please, which way I ought to go from here?"

"That depends a good deal on where you want to get to," said the cat.

"I don't much care where," said Alice.

"Then it doesn't matter which way you go," said the cat.

". . . so long as I get somewhere," Alice added.

"Oh, you're sure to do that," said the cat, "if you only go far enough."

* * *

Now, let us lean back . . . relax . . . and start our imaginary journey. . . .

You've had a pinched nerve in your neck, and the doctor has given you a pill to take, a relaxant, and told you to rest, assuring you that things will improve in time.

At bedtime you stretch out on your back, shut your eyes to rest. You know if you sleep on your back you'll dream, but it's the only way you can be comfortable. You shut your eyes, trying to sleep. The ache lessens. You let your mind wander. Your breathing becomes softer, gentler. You relax. . . .

In your half-sleep you seem to be on a journey. A stranger is walking with you, accompanying you on the journey, "Come," the stranger says, "We can fly. . . ."

Your own voice asks, "Do you have the tickets? I don't seem to
have any."

The stranger laughs. "No. We don't need any tickets. We'll fly by
ourselves."

"Oh, no! No!" you try to say. "I can't fly. I don't know how."

The stranger smiles. "Of course you can. I'll show you. Here, get
in."

You're standing in a grassy airfield. Before you is a small yellow
airplane. The door is open. "Get in," the stranger urges. "You sit on
the left. I'll sit in the right seat."

You get in, protesting that you can't fly . . . that you've never
flown. You look out the window of the plane. There, all along the
field, are a lot of your friends. Are they there to see you make a fool
of yourself? But, they aren't looking at you. They're drinking coffee,
talking and laughing together, not paying attention to you.

The door is shut. The stranger is starting the engine. The propeller
turns, spinning. "Fasten your seat belt," the stranger advises. "Now,"
he adds, "I'm your instructor. . . . You take it off."

You sit there, wondering why you can't leave. The instructor's
voice comes to you. "Put your feet on the rudder pedals. Hold the
wheel with your left hand. With your other hand, pull out the
throttle, that knob there. Slowly. Pull it out—slowly." The engine
roars louder, the plane moves. . . . "Steer down the runway. . . .
Push the wheel forward a little, ever so little. Keep the nose
down. . . . Now, we're going faster. Check your air speed. . . . that
instrument there. Keep the plane straight with your feet. . . . How
fast are we going? 50? 55? 60? 65? Good, now pull back on the wheel,
very gently, very gently. . . . Keep your feet even. . . . We're off the
ground. . . . We're flying. . . . Keep it straight. . . . Keep the air
speed there, steady. . . . We're climbing!

"How does it feel?" asks the instructor. "You took the plane off.
You're actually flying." . . . How does it feel? You've actually taken
off an airplane! Are you frightened? . . . Proud? . . . Worried? . . .
Elated? . . .

You look over at the instructor. He's gazing out the window. "Keep
your eyes moving," he says. "Look around. Look ahead, behind.
Look out each side. Look above, below. Keep your eyes peeled for
other planes. . . ." The instructor shows you how to bank to the
right. "Look before you turn. . . ." You turn the wheel slightly to the
right as you push the right pedal gently. Then you center them each as
you continue the gentle bank. You pull back slightly on the wheel to

keep the nose up, the plane level. You are tense, controlling too much. . . .

You straighten out the turn and fly level, roughly, over–controlling. The instructor says, "Let go of the controls. . . ." You wonder if the instructor is going to take over. He makes no move, but just sits there. "Let go," he commands.

You release the wheel, move your feet off the pedals. The plane continues straight and level. "See," the instructor says, "all you need to do is control it. The plane does the flying by itself. . . ."

You have climbed higher now. Much higher. "I'll show you what happens if you don't *allow* the plane to fly. It needs to maintain a certain air speed. Go below it and the plane stalls." "Pull the wheel back some—like that." You notice the nose go up over the horizon. "Hold it up, push the throttle in. Reduce the engine speed, keep the nose up." The plane slows. . . . The controls are sluggish. . . . It hangs there. . . . It shudders, vibrates. . . . Then the left wing dips. The plane seems to shake, pause, fall. . . .

Suddenly, you are terrified. Now what? What do you do? What is happening? . . . You look at the instructor, your eyes wide in panic. The instructor laughs. . . . "This is a stall." Close to the ground you are dead. Way up here you recover. Pop in the wheel. Hard! Force the nose down—that's right. Level it out with the rudder. You're picking up speed . . . good . . . good. Now lift the nose, put on more power. . . . Keep it level. Now you're flying again. . . ."

Do you feel a sense of relief? . . . You look out. Everything seems to be the same. Sunshine, clouds; you wonder how long you've been flying? . . .

"It's time for your instrument lesson," the instructor says. "Trust your instruments. Trust your instruments. I've shown you how to use them." . . . You can't seem to remember. What instruments? Where are they? . . . A hood covers the seat. You are unable to see outside, unable to see the instructor. All you see is the black instrument panel. . . . You hear the engine droning—did it seem to miss? . . . Is it running faster? It sounds faster. Your thoughts are: Am I diving? I must be. Look at the air speed. It reads the same. What if it's wrong? . . . I'm banking. I know I am banking. I can feel it. I'm banking to the left. Why doesn't the instructor help me? . . . The artificial horizon shows me level. It must be broken. I know I'm turning. I'll correct. Turn the wheel to the right, the right pedal. There. That feels right. But now the horizon shows me turning to the right. I can't be! I feel level. . . . I'm confused. . . ."

The instructor's voice comes to you again, "Trust your instruments. . . ."

You hear a bell dimly—louder. A clock. A clock is awakening you. You reach over numbly to silence it, feeling the pang in your neck and shoulder. A voice says, "Good morning." . . .

When you are ready to share, pool the images, word associations and feelings that come out of this guided meditation. . . .

Guided Meditation on Matthew 17:1–13

"And after six days Jesus took with him Peter and James and John his brother, and led them up a high mountain apart. And he was transfigured before them. . . ." (Matthew 17:1–2a)

Now let us settle back comfortably and close our eyes. . . .

Imagine that you are Peter in about the year 32 A.D. You have been brought up to the top of a high mountain with John and his brother, James, by your friend and teacher, Jesus. It is a hot, dry time of the year, but up here the air is clear, and all is still. What do you see as you look out over the countryside far below? . . . How do you feel about being chosen as one of the three among the twelve disciples to accompany Jesus? . . . What could his reasons be for bringing you up here? . . . Is he going to explain more fully about what he had disclosed to the twelve a week or so ago—that he would suffer much and be put to death, and on the third day be raised from the dead? (What a disturbing and puzzling piece of news that was!) Or could it be something else? . . .

Your reverie is suddenly interrupted by a crackling energy which emanates, materializes, and then finally disappears. But in that time, Jesus is transformed, for you see your master's garment become more brilliantly white, with radiance that is even blinding! What is happening? . . . To add to your amazement, there appear Moses and Elijah; the latter, according to Jewish belief in your time, had never died but had been transported up to heaven. Yet, here they were in all their heavenly glory, talking calmly to Jesus! What can this mean? How marvelous, but also how frightening! You blurt out, "Lord, it is well that we are here; if you wish, I will make three booths here, one for you and one for Moses and one for Elijah." Why did you say that? . . . Was it the first thing that came to your mind? . . . Or was it out of fright? . . . Or did you want to hold onto this glorious moment as long as possible? . . .

As you speak, a bright cloud suddenly overshadows you, and a voice speaks from it, saying, "This is my beloved Son, with whom I am well pleased: listen to him." How do you feel now? . . . To see the glory of God present in Jesus right there before you? (For God had broken through the ordinary, humble daily life of these friends to reveal God's own self in your friend and rabbi!) . . . Jesus comes and touches you, and says, "Rise and have no fear." And when you lift up your eyes you see no one standing with you but Jesus . . . What are you thinking as you and your friends descend down to the plains below, to the work that needs to be done there still?. . . Share whatever images come to your mind. . . .

*   *   *

The faith empowering session where the above guided meditation was given closed with a reading on the transfiguration from Madeleine L'Engle's book, *The Irrational Season*. We add that reading here for its meaning.

> Suddenly they saw him the way he was, the way he really was all the time, although they had never seen it before, the glory which blinds the everyday eye and so becomes invisible. This is how he was, radiant, brilliant, carrying joy like a flaming sun in his hands. This is the way he was—is—from the beginning, and we cannot bear it. So he manned himself, came manifest to us; and there on the mountain they saw him, really saw him, saw his light. . . .[2]

Guided Meditation on Mark 2:1–12

"And when they [four men] could not get near him [Jesus] because of the crowd, they removed the roof above him; and when they had made an opening, they let down the pallet on which the paralytic lay." (Mark 2:4)

I'd like to take your imagination on a camping trip. First, we need to put aside the cares and business of our daily lives. So adjust to a comfortable position. Close your eyes. Wiggle your toes. Shake out any tension that is in your feet. Let go of the tension in your legs. Flex your fingers. Shake out the tension that is in your hands, your arms, your neck, your back. Let your cares drift away, miles away. Focus on your breathing—in and out—in and out. Slow. Regular. Breathing in the quiet—in and out. Slow. Regular. Flow with the breath. . . .

A light breeze brushes your arm. You are at a camp site. It is a warm, sunny, summer morning. You have had two beautiful vacation days so far. It is the third day of your trip. You look around you. Where is this camp site? . . . Who is with you on this trip? . . . One of your companions feels adventurous. You agree to go exploring with this person. You arm yourself with a lunch and with the walkie-talkie that the park ranger gave you. . . . "Communication in case of emergency," he had said. Off you go! Ready or not, ready!

The camp sites are on a dirt road. But the road dead-ends in a woods. You wonder "What is in the woods at the end of the road?" And you wonder again, "What lies beyond the woods?" . . .

There is no real path in the woods, but it looks so inviting! Your companion, the poet (Robert Frost), recalls:

> Two roads diverged in a wood, and I—
> I took the one less traveled by,
> And that has made all the difference.[3]

Lunch and walkie-talkie in hand, you head into the woods. How does it feel, entering this pathless woods? . . .

It is an old woods, the trees are dense and tall. The leaves are a deep summer green. The sun is warm as it peeks between the trees. There is a coolness in the shade. The sky is bright blue. Ah! Smell the pine trees. What do you hear? . . . Chirping birds? Frogs? A brook? Squirrels teasingly chasing each other? What is it like in this woods? . . .

You look back. You no longer can see the road. How does that make you feel? . . .

You continue to walk on. Exploring. The ground has become more hilly. A carpet of pine needles. Patches of bright green moss. Beautiful! But, whoops! A tree trunk you didn't see. You're falling! You struggle to catch yourself. Your foot slips on the moss. Thunk! You are down, lying on your back. A hard fall. Pain shoots down your spine. Your legs are numb. You try to get up. But you can't. You can't! . . . You are lying there, unable to move!

Your companion tries to help you up. It doesn't work. Perhaps this person tries to carry you. Your back hurts too much. You are stuck. How are you feeling as your friend struggles to help you? . . . What images and thoughts do you have? . . .

Your companion radios on the walkie-talkie for help. An unknown voice responds. It offers the services of a helicopter to take you to the local hospital. A helicopter! "Safest way out of the woods for back problems," the voice responds. You lie in wait for the helicopter. What do you think/feel? . . . Look around the woods as you wait. The trees, the birds. What do you see? . . . Where is your companion? . . .

A motor. The helicopter hovers overhead. It cannot land in the woods because of the denseness of the trees. A stretcher is being lowered through a small space between tree branches. A stretcher, slowly descending from the helicopter. What is it made of? . . . Does it look strong? . . . Soon you will be strapped in this stretcher, your companion far below you, the helicopter waiting above you. Imagine how that will feel! . . .

There is no choice. Can you trust the stretcher? . . . The helicopter crew and doctor are experienced. "Best in the country," says the park ranger.

The stretcher descends. It is 15 feet from the ground now. The stretcher rocks in the gentle breeze. What are you thinking? . . . What images come to your mind? . . . How do you feel? . . . What will happen? . . .

It is time now to share the images that flow from this guided meditation . . . .

Guided Meditation on Mark 14:26–42

"And they [Jesus and the disciples] went to a place which was called Gethsemane; and he said to his disciples, 'Sit here, while I pray.' . . . And he came and found them sleeping. . . ." (Mark 14:32, 37a)

[Have group get comfortable, close eyes, breathe deeply, several times, relax feet, limbs, hands, and arms. . . .]

Now allow your mind to wander as we live some moments as followers of the teacher, the master, even Jesus.

You have had a strange supper together with the others, a long supper, a Passover meal with conversation and prayers and wine. Finally, with the hour late, later than usual, you are led by the master out into the cooler night air—led to the Mount of Olives. As you walk, you hear Jesus say, "You will all fall from your faith. . . ." And you hear the big fisherman scoff and object, "Maybe everyone else will fall away, but not I! Even if I must die with you, Jesus, I will never disown you!". . . . And the others agree and say the same thing—John agrees with Peter—and Andrew also. . . . And you— how do *you* respond? . . . Does Jesus doubt how you feel? . . . How *do* you feel? . . .

You walk on in silence until you come to the garden—the garden called Gethsemane—and Jesus says, "Sit here while I pray." He beckons to Peter and to John and to you and bids you follow him further. And you go in his footsteps, suddenly aware of the late hour and your exhaustion. Then Jesus pauses and says to the three of you, "My heart is ready to break with grief; stop here, and stay awake."

You sit on the sandy soil and watch as your master goes a stone's throw further and kneels to pray. You have seen the look of pain on his face. You lean back and then lie back. You see the stars in the black night. It is so late—you are so tired. How many cups of wine have you had? . . . It always makes you feel drowsy. . . . It's been such a week: the parade into Jerusalem, the crowds shouting, hailing your teacher, calling him a king! What a day that was! So many people—so much walking—so much confusion. And the next day in the temple when he turned out the merchants: had you ever seen him so dismayed, so angry? The priests—they themselves were furious. It was good to get out of the city that night, good to get out and rest, and rest. . . .

Suddenly you are jolted by the sound of his voice, "Asleep, Simon? Were you not able to stay awake for one hour?"

His eyes move to John and then to you stretched out on the ground. "Stay awake, all of you; and pray that you may be spared the test. The spirit is willing, but the flesh is weak!"

You say nothing. You stare at the sky—the blackness and the thousands of stars—as Jesus moves back to his prayers. How do *you* feel from the sting of his barbs? . . . Why is it so bad to get some sleep, you wonder? You're so tired. The week has been so long—so many, many times of teaching, stories, parables. And the way he withered the fig tree! That was so strange. Jesus wanted figs! It's not even the season! Why would he take it out on the tree? . . . It was so strange. . . . And all that talk about the temple being destroyed and built up in three days—what did the master mean? Oh, it's so good to lie back, to relax. . . .

Again, you are startled by Jesus' voice—not so angry as hurt that again you had slept. Neither John, nor Peter, nor you respond. Like children you remain silent. And your thoughts turn to the Passover meal. . . . It was good to celebrate it together, to share the bread and

SCRIPTURE AND IMAGINATION 111

the wine. . . . You recall that he had said that one of the group was
going to betray him. . . . And what did he mean by breaking the
bread? . . . What had he said? "This is my body, broken for you."
And when he poured the wine: "This is my blood, the blood of the
new covenant." What a strange statement? . . . the wine. . . . the
bread. . . . It was a good . . . it was a strange . . . meal; and it is so
good now in the fresh air . . . relaxing . . . relaxing. . . .

Then you are startled again: "Still sleeping? Still taking your ease?
Enough! The hour has come!" . . .

Now, with your eyes still closed, share with us some of the images
you have seen or felt. When it seems the right time I will call the
group back together. But for now share your images. . . .

Guided Meditation on Luke 9:62

"Jesus said to him, 'No one who puts his hand to the plow and looks
back is fit for the kingdom of God.'" (Luke 9:62)

[Get the group to relax, close their eyes, breathe deeply.]

Come with me to a faraway country a long time ago. It is Palestine
in mid-November. . . .

"Reuben, Reuben, wake up. . . . It is time!" You hear the voice
calling. . . . How can it be time? Time for what? . . . "Reuben, get
up!" The voice is louder and more insistent. A hand grasps your
shoulder and shakes you. You open your eyes. It is still dark, but
your father is standing over you, and suddenly you remember that
this is the day. Today it is to be your turn at last.

You scramble off your straw pallet and fumble for your sandals in
the dimness. Where are they? You will need them. Throwing on your
tunic you hurry to get ready. How could you oversleep on this special
day, the day for which you have waited for so long?

You roll up your pallet and store it in the corner of the room. Your
missing sandals were under it on the floor. Your mother hands you
your lunch, for it will be a long day in the fields. You are wide awake
now and filled with excitement.

Your brothers are waiting outside. The oxen are yoked and ready.
You take a piece of bread and some olives to eat on the way. You are
ready. . . . Are you really ready? . . .

It seemed this day would never come. The fall rains went on and
on. But at last they have stopped. Now the ground is soft, and it is

time to plow and sow. This year, father has promised that you can help with the plowing!

Your father is one of many farmers in this region. He owns his own field and tends it with great care, and he even has a team of oxen. Each year you have tried to help. Last year you carried and pulled rocks and stones to get the field ready. How your arms and back ached! How could there be so many of them left in the field when you had all worked so hard before? You also helped your mother and your sisters to do the sowing, being oh, so careful, not to waste any seeds of flax, barley, and wheat.

Day after day you have gone to the fields as the sun is coming up. Each time you have hoped that you could help with the plowing. This is such a crucial step. . . . The plow must go just so deep, or the crop will not grow and the land will not produce. The crop is so important. . . . Without it, how will the taxes be paid? . . . What will you eat? . . . How will you live? . . .

At last you reach the field. Your father carefully takes the plow and fastens it to the yoke. The oxen wait patiently. The handle of the plow is worn smooth from use. And the blade must be held correctly so that it will make a furrow from 3 to 5 inches deep. It must be done just right. You have watched and watched your father and brothers do it, and you are almost certain that you can do it, too.

But, as you wait, you wonder. . . .

Am I really big enough and strong enough after all? . . . Can I guide the plow? . . . The furrows *must* be straight. Will it be too heavy? . . . . What if the furrow is too deep, or not deep enough? . . . What will the plow feel like? . . .

Then it is time. . . . You grasp the handle in your right hand, tightly. You mustn't drop it. Father places the goad in your left hand, so that you can guide the oxen. How huge they are. . . . How strong. . . . You touch them gently with the goad and begin the first furrow, trying to remember all you have learned: Don't use the goad too much or you won't be able to manage the oxen. Stroke them gently. Keep moving. No stopping in the middle. Above all, *no* looking back, if your furrow is to be straight. . . .

How do you know? . . . How can you tell? . . . Is the furrow too deep? . . . Is it too shallow? . . . Are there still some rocks in the way? . . .

It feels as if the oxen are pulling you along—too fast, too fast. How can you possibly hold the plow straight? Let up a little and slow down, slow down. . . . Well, not *that* slow! Why won't they pay attention to you? . . . Wait, wait. . . . You have dropped the goad. . . . Stop, stop! But the oxen plod on. The plow is in your hand. You can't look for the goad. You *must* keep your eyes on that tree at the end of the field. What are you thinking? . . . How can you guide the team now? . . .

The sun grows hotter. The dirt covers your feet. Bits of dust get in your eyes. You are so thirsty. . . . The edge of the field is so far away. . . . How do you feel? . . .

One question burns in your mind: *Is* the furrow straight? How you ache to look back to see. Perhaps just a quick peek. . . . surely you can chance that without losing control. . . . You start to turn. Just then you hear your father's voice calling, "Look ahead, look ahead. . . ."

With your father's voice echoing in your ears, can you share the feelings and images which have been coming to mind in you as you have entered into this guided meditation? . . .

Guided Meditation on Luke 15:11–24

"And he [Jesus] said, 'There was a man who had two sons; and the younger of them said to his father, "Father, give me the share of property that falls to me." And he divided his living between them. Not many days later, the younger son gathered all he had and took his journey into a far country, and there he squandered his property in loose living.' " (Luke 15:11–13).

Close your eyes, if you will, and relax. Let the cares of your day wash off your body, as though you were standing in a shower. Feel the cleansing "water" flowing over you. . . . now concentrate on your breathing. Breathe in. . . . Breathe out. . . . As you breathe in, feel a sense of peace invading your body, reaching down into every corner. As you breathe out, release the anxieties you have brought with you. Breathe in. . . . Breathe out. . . . Let yourself be held in the Spirit of Christ. . . .

Imagine now that you are a woman living a long time ago in Palestine. You have a husband and two sons. Your life is busy, for the lives of everyone in those days were busy, just trying to make a living. *Your* family life is a bit easier than for most, for you live on a large farm with hired servants. But still there is much to keep you oc-cupied. As a woman, however, you are not consulted in the big decisions of the family. But you hear what is going on. And you have feelings.

One day your younger son, your "baby," comes in to talk with your husband: "Father," he says, "give me the share of property that falls to me." Thoughts and emotions race through your mind. Why does he want that property? Why now? . . . What is he going to do with it? Is he going to leave home? Leave you? . . . What are you feeling as these thoughts come to you? . . .

Sure enough, your younger son packs his bags and gets ready to travel. All he will say to you is that he is going to a far country. You give him a hug. And then you watch as he sets off down the road, growing smaller and smaller against the hot, dry sky. What are you feeling now? . . .

The months pass. Or are they years? Life settles into a new routine. The busyness of the farm claims your attention. Your older son is there with you, working hard—day in, day out. Occasionally you hear news from travellers about life in the far countries out there. One day you hear of a drought, and a famine. You think of your younger son, wondering how he is. Get in touch with your feelings as you wonder. . . .

Then, one day, as the sun beats down relentlessly from that middle-Eastern sky, you happen to look up towards the road. There, over in the distance, you see a tiny figure coming towards you. Who is it? The figure draws closer. You imagine that you can recognize the walk, for you have seen it many, many times. Can it be? Just then your husband comes running by, heading down the road towards that approaching figure. You hadn't known that he was looking in that same direction, too. You hadn't realized how many times you—and he—had looked down that same road over the past years. And now your husband is running. Can you remember when the last time was that you saw your husband running? . . .

Suddenly you find yourself filled with anxiety. What will your husband do? If it *is* your younger son coming up that road, what will his father do to him? You think that you know your husband well, but a surge of doubt comes up within you. Get in touch with your feelings. . . .

The two figures draw closer. They are too far away for you to hear them, but you can see them clearly: the one walking slowly towards you, head bowed; the other running, head up. Then it happens! Your husband reaches your son, and in a moment of glorious abandon, father picks up son and swings him round and round in a joyous embrace! What are you feeling now? . . . The memories of these past years come flooding back. And the many emotions. All you can see is a father lifting a son in joyful abandon. What could your husband be feeling? . . . and your younger son? . . . Most importantly for you, what are *you* feeling? . . .

When you are in touch with your feelings, share them openly in the group, if you will, along with any images and word pictures that they bring with them into your mind. . . .

Notes

3/Sharing and Prayer
1. Dr. Seuss (Geisel, Theodor Seuss), "What Was I Scared Of?" in *The Sneetches and Other Stories* (New York: Random House, 1961).

4/Presenting Our Stories
1. Hans-Georg Gadamer, *Truth and Method*. The translation was edited by Garrett Barden and John Cumming. (New York: The Seabury Press, A Continuum Book, 1975; originally published as *Wahrheit und Methode,* Tubingen; J.C.B. Mohr [Paul Siebeck], 1960), p. 269.
2. *Ibid.,* p. 271.

5/Exploring God's Word
1. Sharon Lea Parks, *The Critical Years: The Young Adult Search for a Faith to Live By* (San Francisco: Harper & Row, 1986), pp. 120–122. Parks builds on the earlier work of Princeton's James Loder, substituting the simpler word, "pause" for his longer phrase, "interlude for scanning;" see James E. Loder, *The Transforming Moment: Understanding Convictional Experiences* (San Francisco: Harper & Row, 1981), p. 32.
2. George M. Prince, *The Practice of Creativity: A Manual for Dynamic Group Problem Solving* (New York: Collier Books, A Division of Macmillan Publishing Co., Inc., 1970), p. 83.
3. Urban T. Holmes, III, *Ministry and Imagination* (New York: The Seabury Press, 1976), p. 107.
4. Harold Rugg, *Imagination* (New York: Harper & Row, 1963), p. 39.
5. See for example, *Gospel Parallels: A Synopsis of the First Three Gospels,* edited by Burton H. Throckmorton, Jr. (Toronto: Thomas Nelson & Sons, 1949).
6. Gadamer, *Truth and Method,* p. 269.
7. Prince, *The Practice of Creativity,* p. 85.
8. One such commentary is *The Interpreter's Bible* (New York: Abingdon Press, 1951). *The Interpreter's Bible* comes in twelve volumes; the commentary, or middle section on each page, was edited by George Arthur Buttrick.

6/Imagining and Imaging
1. Loder, *The Transforming Moment,* p. 18.
2. Holmes, *Ministry and Imagination,* p. 102.

3. *Ibid.*, p. 56.
4. Parks, *The Critical Years,* p. 115.
5. William F. Lynch, S.J., *Images of Faith: An Exploration of the Ironic Imagination* (South Bend: University of Notre Dame Press, 1973), pages 17 and 5.
6. Holmes, *Ministry and Imagination,* p. 88.

7/Making Connections
1. Gadamer, *Truth and Method,* p. 269.
2. For a more detailed treatment of this question, see Anthony C. Thiselton, *The Two Horizons: New Testament Hermeneutics and Philosophical Description* (Grand Rapids, Michigan: William B. Eerdmans Publishing Company, 1980).
3. Gadamer, *Truth and Method,* p. 264.
4. *Ibid.*, p. 273.
5. *Ibid.*, p. 263.
6. Bultmann focusses on the mythological elements in the biblical horizon, which he sees as unnecessary stumbling blocks to modern understanding and faith. His method of interpretation seeks to "recover the deeper meaning behind the mythological conceptions"; he believes that the deeper meaning is best expressed to the modern world in the terms of existentialist philosophy. See Rudolf Bultmann, *Jesus Christ and Mythology* (New York: Charles Scribner's Sons, 1958), especially p. 18.
7. Paul Ricoeur, *The Symbolism of Evil,* trans. Emerson Buchanan; Religious Perspectives 17, planned, edited by Ruth Nanda Ashen (New York: Harper and Row, 1967), p. 351.

8/Drawing Implications
1. Lawrence LeShan, *How to Meditate: A Guide to Self-Discovery* (Toronto: Bantam Books, 1974), p. 18.

10/The Meaning Behind the Method
1. See Thomas Groome, *Christian Religious Education: Sharing Our Story and Vision* (San Francisco: Harper and Row, 1980).
2. Walter Wink, *The Bible in Human Transformation: Toward a New Paradigm for Biblical Study* (Philadelphia: Fortress Press, 1973). See also: *Transforming Bible Study: A Leader's Guide* (Nashville: Abingdon Press, 1980).
3. William Beaven Abernethy and Philip Joseph Mayher, "Faith Horizons and Images: A Theory and Practice for Empowering Faith." Doctor of Ministry Thesis, Andover Newton Theological School, 1983.
4. Harvey Cox, *Religion in the Secular City: Toward a Postmodern Theology* (New York: Simon & Schuster, Inc., A Touchstone Book, 1984), p. 123.
5. Robert Kegan, "There the Dance Is: Religious Dimensions of a Developmental Perspective" *Toward Moral and Religious Maturity* (Morristown, New Jersey: Silver Burdett Co., 1980), pp. 403–440, especially pp. 411 ff.
6. Robert Kegan, *The Evolving Self: Problem and Process in Human Development* (Cambridge, Massachusetts: Harvard University Press, 1982), p. 107.
7. Wilfred Cantwell Smith, *Faith and Belief* (Princeton, New Jersey: Princeton University Press, 1979), p. 118.
8. Herbert Fingarette, *The Self in Transformation: Psychoanalysis, Philosophy, and the Life of the Spirit* (New York: Harper and Row, 1963), p. 63.
9. Parks, *The Critical Years,* p. 115.
10. Smith, p. 158.
11. James Fowler, *Stages of Faith: The Psychology of Human Development and the Quest for Meaning* (San Francisco: Harper and Row, 1981), pp. 172–3.

12. Kegan, pp. 184ff.
13. John H. Westerhoff, III, *Will Our Children Have Faith?* (New York: The Seabury Press—A Crossroad Book, 1976), p. 89.
14. E.C. Lathem, ed., *The Poetry of Robert Frost* (New York: Holt, Reinhart, and Winston, 1969), p. 34.
15. Kegan, p. 191ff.
16. Fowler, p. 173.
17. *Ibid.*, pp. 182–3.
18. Kegan, pp. 221ff.
19. Fowler, p. 179.
20. Westerhoff, p. 89.
21. Harold S. Kushner, *When Bad Things Happen to Good People* (New York: Schocken Books, 1981).
22. Kegan, pp. 259–260.
23. *Ibid.*, pages 115 and 121.
24. *Ibid.*, p. 244.
25. Fowler, pp. 197–8.
26. Kegan, pp. 103ff.
27. Fowler, p. 186.
28. Ricoeur, p. 349.
29. Ronald Marstin, *Beyond Our Tribal Gods: The Maturing of Faith* (Maryknoll, New York: Orbis Books, 1979), pp. 36–37.
30. *Ibid.*, p. 54.
31. *Ibid.*, p. 110.
32. Fowler, p. 273.
33. Murray Stein, *Jung's Treatment of Christianity: The Psychotherapy of a Religious Tradition* (Wilmette, Illinois; Chiron Publications, 1985), pages 23, 41.

13/Praying the Word
1. From *The New English Bible, New Testament.* © The Delegates of the Oxford University Press and the Syndics of the Cambridge University Press 1961. Reprinted by permission.
2. Madeleine L'Engle, *The Irrational Season.* (New York: The Seabury Press, A Crossroad Book, 1977), p. 194.
3. E.C. Lathem, ed., *The Poetry of Robert Frost*, p. 105.

Bibliography

Christian Education

Boys, Mary C. *Biblical Interpretation in Religious Education*. Birmingham, Alabama: Religious Education Press, 1980.

Campbell, Joseph, ed. *Myths, Dreams and Religion*. New York: E.P. Dutton & Co., 1970.

Dykstra, Craig. *Vision and Character: A Christian Educator's Alternative to Kohlberg*. New York: Paulist Press, 1981.

Freire, Paulo. *Pedagogy of the Oppressed*. New York: Herder and Herder. 1970.

Fromm, Erich. *To Have or to Be?* New York: Bantam Books, 1981.

Girardot, Norman, and Ricketts, MacLinscott. *Imagination and Meaning: The Scholarly and Literary Worlds of Mircea Eliade*. New York: Seabury Press, 1982.

Groome, Thomas H. *Christian Religious Education: Sharing Our Story and Vision*. San Francisco: Harper and Row, 1980.

Harris, Maria. *The D.R.E. Book: Questions and Strategies for Parish Personnel*. New York: The Paulist Press, 1976.

Harris, Maria. "From Myth to Parable: Language and Religious Education." *Religious Education* 73, no. 4, July–August, 1978, pp. 387–398.

Harris, Maria. *Portrait of Youth Ministry*. New York: The Paulist Press, 1981.

Harris, Maria. *Teaching and Religious Imagination*. San Francisco: Harper and Row, 1987.

Hauerwas, Stanley. *Vision and Virtue: Essays in Christian Ethical Reflection*. South Bend, Indiana: Fides Publishing Co., 1974.

Kelsey, Morton. *Can Christians Be Educated?* Mishawaka, Indiana: Religious Education Press, Inc., 1977.

Kelsey, Morton. *Myth, History and Faith*. New York: The Paulist Press, 1974.

Loder, James E. *The Transforming Moment: Understanding Convictional Experiences*. San Francisco: Harper and Row, 1981.

Loder, James E. "Transformation in Religious Education." *Religious Education* 76, no. 2, March–April 1981, pp. 204–221.

McClendon, James. *Biography as Theology*. Nashville: Abingdon Press, 1974.

Meland, Bernard E. *Fallible Forms and Symbols*. Philadelphia: Fortress Press, 1976.

Moran, Gabriel. *Design for Religion*. New York: Herder and Herder, 1970.

Moran, Gabriel. *Education Toward Adulthood*. New York: The Paulist Press, 1979.

Moran, Gabriel. *Interplay: A Theory of Religion and Education*. Winona, Minnesota: Saint Mary's Press, Christian Brothers Publishing, 1981.

Noel, Daniel C., ed. *Echoes of the Wordless Word*. Missoula, Montana: Printing Department, University of Montana, American Academy of Religion, Society of Biblical Literature, 1973.

O'Hare, Padraic. *Foundations of Religious Education*. New York: The Paulist Press, 1978.

O'Hare, Padraic. *Tradition and Transformation in Religious Education*. Birmingham, Alabama: Religious Education Press, 1979.

Panikkar, R. *Myth, Faith and Hermeneutics*. New York: The Paulist Press, 1979.

Robinson, Edward. *The Original Vision*. New York: Seabury Press, 1983.

Ross-Bryant, Lynn. *Imagination and the Life of the Spirit*. Chico, California: Scholars Press, 1981.

Shea, John. *Stories of Faith*. Chicago, Illinois: The Thomas More Press, 1980.

Taylor, Marvin J., ed. *An Introduction to Christian Education*. Nashville, Tennessee: Abingdon Press, 1966.

Taylor, Marvin J., ed. *Foundations for Christian Education in an Era of Change*. Nashville, Tennessee: Abingdon Press, 1976.

Westerhoff, John H., III. *Inner Growth, Outer Change: An Educational Guide to Church Renewal*. New York: Seabury Press—A Crossroad Book, 1979.

Westerhoff, John H., III. *Who Are We? The Quest for a Religious Education*. Birmingham, Alabama: Religious Education Press, 1978.

Westerhoff, John H., III. *Will Our Children Have Faith?* New York: The Seabury Press—A Crossroad Book, 1976.

Whitehead, Alfred North. *The Aims of Education*. London: Williams and Northgate, 1932.

Faith Development

Abernethy, William Beaven, and Mayher, Philip Joseph. "Faith Horizons and Images: A Theory and Practice for Empowering Faith." Doctor of Ministry Thesis, Andover Newton Theological School, 1983.

Berrigan, Daniel, and Coles, Robert. *The Geography of Faith: Conversations Between Daniel Berrigan When Underground, and Robert Coles*. Boston: Beacon Press, 1971.

Dykstra, Craig R. "Theological Table Talk: Transformation in Faith and Morals." *Theology Today*, Vol. XXXIX, April 1982, pp. 56–64.

Erikson, Erik H., ed. *Adulthood*. New York: W.W. Norton & Co., 1978.

Fingarette, Herbert. *The Self in Transformation: Psychoanalysis, Philosophy, and the Life of the Spirit*. New York: Harper and Row, 1963.

Fowler, James, and Keen, Sam. *Life Maps: Conversations on the Journey of Faith*, edited by Jerome Berryman. Waco, Texas: Winston Press, 1978.

Fowler, James W. *Becoming Adult, Becoming Christian: Adult Development and Christian Faith*. San Francisco: Harper & Row, 1984.

Fowler, James W. *Faith Development and Pastoral Care*. Theology and Pastoral Care, Browning, Don S., editor. Philadelphia: The Fortress Press, 1987.

Fowler, James. *Stages of Faith: The Psychology of Human Development and the Quest for Meaning*. San Francisco: Harper and Row, 1981.

Gilligan, Carol. "In a Different Voice: Women's Conception of the Self and of Morality." *Harvard Educational Review* Vol. 47, no. 4, 1977, pp. 481–517.

Gilligan, Carol. *In a Different Voice: Psychological Theory and Women's Development*. Cambridge, Massachusetts: Harvard University Press, 1982.

Gilligan, Carol. "Woman's Place in Man's Life Cycle." *Harvard Educational Review* 49, no. 4 (1979): pp. 431–446.

Groome, Thomas H. *Christian Religious Education: Sharing our Story and Vision.* San Francisco: Harper and Row, 1980.

Hillman, James. *Insearch: Psychology and Religion.* New York: Charles Scribner's Sons, 1967.

Kegan, Robert. *The Evolving Self: Problem and Process in Human Development.* Cambridge, Massachusetts: Harvard University Press, 1982.

Kegan, Robert G. "There the Dance Is: Religious Dimensions of a Developmental Perspective." *Toward Moral and Religious Maturity: The First International Conference on Moral and Religious Development.* Senior authors: James W. Fowler and Antoine Vergote. Morristown, New Jersey: Silver Burdett Company, 1980: pp. 403–440.

Kohlberg, Lawrence. *The Philosophy of Moral Development.* San Francisco: Harper and Row, 1981.

Kohlberg, Lawrence. "Stage and Sequence." *Handbook of Socialization,* D. Goslin, ed. New York: Rand McNally, 1968.

Levinson, Daniel J., with Darrow, Charlotte N., Klein, Edward B., Levinson, Maria H., and McKee, Braxton. *The Seasons of a Man's Life.* New York: Ballantine Books, 1978.

Lickona, Thomas, ed. *Moral Development and Behavior: Theory, Research, and Social Issues.* New York: Holt, Rinehart and Winston, 1976.

Loder, James E. *The Transforming Moment: Understanding Convictional Experiences.* San Francisco: Harper and Row, 1981.

Loder, James. "Transformation in Christian Education." *Religious Education* 76, no. 2 (March–April 1981): pp. 204–221.

Marstin, Ronald. *Beyond our Tribal Gods: The Maturing of Faith.* Maryknoll, New York: Orbis Books, 1979.

Niebuhr, H. Richard. *Radical Monotheism and Western Culture.* New York: Harper Torchbooks, 1943.

Parks, Sharon Lea. *The Critical Years: The Young Adult Search for a Faith to Live By.* San Francisco: Harper & Row, 1986.

Parks, Sharon Lea. "Faith Development and Imagination in the Context of Higher Education." Th.D. Dissertation, Harvard Divinity School, 1980.

Piaget, Jean. *The Moral Judgment of the Child.* New York: The Free Press, 1965.

Piaget, Jean. *Six Psychological Studies.* Translated by Anita Tenzer; translation edited by David Elkind; introduction, notes, glossary by David Elkind. New York: Random House, 1967.

Singer, Dorothy G., and Revenson, Tracey A. *A Piaget Primer: How a Child Thinks.* New York: A Plume Book, New American Library, 1978.

Sheehy, Gail. *Passages: Predictable Crises of Adult Life.* New York: E.P. Dutton, 1974, 1976.

Smith, Wilfred Cantwell. *Faith and Belief.* Princeton, New Jersey: Princeton University Press, 1979.

Stein, Murray. *Jung's Treatment of Christianity: The Psychotherapy of a Religious Tradition.* Chiron Publications, Wilmette, Illinois, 1985.

Tillich, Paul. *Theology of Culture.* Edited by Robert C. Kimball. New York: Oxford University Press, 1959.

Hermeneutics

Abernethy, William Beaven, and Mayher, Philip Joseph. "Faith Horizons and Images: A Theory and Practice for Empowering Faith." Doctor of Ministry Thesis,

Andover Newton Theological School, 1983.

Bultmann, Rudolf. *Jesus Christ and Mythology.* New York: Charles Scribner's Sons, 1958.

Bultmann, Rudolf, and Five Critics. *Kerygma and Myth: A Theological Debate.* Eidted by Hans Werner Bartsch; articles by H.W. Bartsch, Austin Farrer, Ernst Lohmeyer, Julius Schniewind, and Helmut Thielicke. New York: Harper Torchbooks/The Cloister Library, Harper & Brothers, 1961.

Crossan, John Dominic. *Cliffs of Fall: Paradox and Polyvalence in the Parables of Jesus.* New York: The Seabury Press—A Crossroad Book, 1980.

Farrer, Austin. *The Glass of Vision: Bampton Lectures for 1948.* Glasgow: The University Press, 1948.

Gadamer, Hans-Georg. *Truth and Method.* The translation was edited by Barden, Garrett, and Cumming, John. New York: The Seabury Press—A Continuum Book, 1975. (Originally published as *Wahrheit und Methode*, Tubingen; J.C.B. Mohr [Paul Siebeck], 1960.)

Gospel Parallels: A Synopsis of the First Three Gospels, edited by Burton H. Throckmorton, Jr. Toronto: Thomas Nelson & Sons, 1949.

The Interpreter's Bible, in Twelve Volumes, edited by George Arthur Buttrick, Walter Russell Bowie, John Knox, Nolan B. Harmon, Paul Scherer, and Samuel Terrien. New York: Abingdon Press, 1951.

Jensen, Richard A. *Telling the Story: Variety and Imagination in Preaching.* Minneapolis: Augsburg Publishing House, 1980.

Kelsey, David H. *The Uses of Scripture in Recent Theology.* Philadelphia: Fortress Press, 1975.

Ricoeur, Paul. *Essays on Biblical Interpretation.* Edited with an Introduction by Lewis S. Mudge. Philadelphia: Fortress Press, 1980.

Ricoeur, Paul. *The Symbolism of Evil.* Translated by Emerson Buchanan; Religious Perspectives 17, planned and edited by Ruth Nanda Ashen. New York: Harper & Row, 1967.

Rogers, Jack, Editor. *Biblical Authority.* Waco, Texas: Word Books, 1977.

Thiselton, Anthony C. *The Two Horizons: New Testament Hermeneutics and Philosophical Description.* Grand Rapids, Michigan: William B. Eerdmans Publishing Company, 1980.

Tillich, Paul. *Systematic Theology, Volume I.* London: Nisbet & Co., Ltd., 1953. Copyright U.S.A., University of Chicago Press, 1951.

Tracy, David. *Blessed Rage for Order: The New Pluralism in Theology.* New York: The Seabury Press—A Crossroad Book, 1975.

Tracy, David. *The Analogical Imagination: Christian Theology and the Culture of Pluralism.* New York: Crossroad, 1981.

Trible, Phyllis. *God and the Rhetoric of Sexuality.* Philadelphia: Fortress Press, 1978.

Wink, Walter. *The Bible in Human Transformation: Toward a New Paradigm for Biblical Study.* Philadelphia: Fortress Press, 1973.

Wink, Walter. *Transforming Bible Study: A Leader's Guide.* Nashville: Abingdon Press, 1980.

Imagination

Abernethy, William Beaven. *A New Look for Sunday Morning.* Nashville: Abingdon Press, 1975.

Abernethy, William Beaven, and Mayher, Philip Joseph. "Faith Horizons and Images: A Theory and Practice for Empowering Faith." Doctor of Ministry Thesis, Andover Newton Theological School, 1983.

Bettelheim, Bruno. *The Uses of Enchantment: The Meaning and Importance of Fairy Tales.* New York: Alfred A. Knopf, 1976.

Bunyan, John. *The Pilgrim's Progress.* The first part was originally published in 1678; reprint paperback edition: New York: The Pocket Library, Pocket Books, Inc., 1957.

Clark, Linda; Ronan, Marian; and Walker, Eleanor. *Image-Breaking/Image-Building: A Handbook for Creative Worship with Women of Christian Tradition.* New York: The Pilgrim Press, 1981.

Craddock, Fred B. *As One Without Authority.* Nashville: Abingdon Press, 1971.

The Poetry of Robert Frost. Lathem, E.C., ed. New York: Holt, Rinehart, and Winston, 1969.

Harris, Maria. *Teaching and Religious Imagination.* San Francisco: Harper and Row, 1987.

L'Engle, Madeleine. *The Irrational Season.* New York: The Seabury Press—A Crossroad Book, 1977.

LeShan, Lawrence. *How to Meditate: A Guide to Self-Discovery.* Toronto: Bantam Books, 1974.

Loder, James E. *The Transforming Moment: Understanding Convictional Experiences.* San Francisco: Harper & Row, 1981.

Loder, James E. "Transformation in Christian Education." *Religious Education* 76, no. 2 (1981): pp. 204–221.

Lynch, William F. *Images of Faith: An Exploration of the Ironic Imagination.* South Bend: University of Notre Dame Press, 1973.

Minear, Paul S. *Images of the Church in the New Testament.* Philadelphia: The Westminster Press, 1960.

Mitchell, Henry H. *The Recovery of Preaching.* San Francisco: Harper & Row, 1977.

Niebuhr, H. Richard. *The Meaning of Revelation.* New York: The Macmillan Company, 1960.

Parks, Sharon Lea. *The Critical Years: The Young Adult Search for a Faith to Live By.* San Francisco: Harper & Row, 1986.

Parks, Sharon Lea. "Faith Development and Imagination in the Context of Higher Education." Th.D. Dissertation, Harvard Divinity School, 1980.

Prince, George M. *The Practice of Creativity: A Manual for Dynamic Group Problem Solving.* New York: Collier Books, A Division of Macmillan Publishing Co., Inc. 1970.

Rugg, Harold. *Imagination.* New York: Harper & Row, 1963.

Dr. Seuss (Geisel, Theodor Seuss). "What Was I Scared Of?" in *The Sneetches and Other Stories.* New York: Random House, 1961.

Shea, John. *Stories of Faith.* Chicago, Illinois: The Thomas More Press, 1980.

Wheelwright, Philip. *The Burning Fountain: A Study in the Language of Symbolism.* Bloomington: Indiana University Press, 1968.

Ministry and the Church

Anderson, James D., and Jones, Ezra Earl. *The Management of Ministry: Leadership, Purpose, Structure, Community.* San Francisco: Harper & Row, 1978.

Bennett, John C. *The Radical Imperative: From Theology to Social Ethics.* Philadelphia: The Westminster Press, 1975.

Bianchi, Eugene C., and Ruether, Rosemary Radford. *From Machismo to Mutuality: Essays on Sexism and Woman-Man Liberation.* New York: Paulist Press, 1976.

Biersdorf, John E. *Hunger for Experience: Vital Religious Communities in America.* New York: The Seabury Press—A Crossroad Book, 1975.

Boff, Leonardo. *Jesus Christ Liberator: A Critical Christology for Our Time*. Mary-knoll, New York: Orbis Books, 1979.

Bonhoeffer, Dietrich. *Life Together*. Translated and with an Introduction by John W. Doberstein. New York: Harper & Row, 1954.

Broholm, Richard, and Hoffman, John. "Empowering Laity for their Full Ministry: A Workbook from the Laity Project." Editing and Revision by Janet Madore. Unpublished. Newton Centre, Massachusetts: Andover Newton Laity Project, 1981.

Broholm, Richard. "Toward Claiming and Identifying Our Ministry in the Work-place." *Laity Project Newsletter* 3, #3 (Spring/Summer 1982): pp. 1–11.

Brown, Robert McAfee. *Theology in a New Key: Responding to Liberation Themes*. Philadelphia: The Westminster Press, 1978.

Browning, Don. S. *The Moral Context of Pastoral Care*. Philadelphia: The West-minster Press, 1976.

Calian, Carnegie Samuel. *Today's Pastor in Tomorrow's World*. New York: Hawthorn Books, Inc., 1977.

Cobb, John B., Jr. *Christ in a Pluralistic Age*. Philadelphia: The Westminster Press, 1975.

Cox, Harvey. *Religion in the Secular City: Toward a Postmodern Theology*. New York: Simon & Schuster, Inc., A Touchstone Book, 1984.

Dulles, Avery, S.J. *Models of the Church: A Critical Assessment of The Church in All Its Aspects*. Garden City, New York: Doubleday & Company, Inc., 1974.

"Education for Ministry: A Program of Theological Education by Extension." Unpublished. Sewanee, Tennessee: The School of Theology, The University of the South, 1977.

Fackre, Gabriel. *The Christian Story: A Narrative Interpretation of Basic Christian Doctrine*. Grand Rapids, Michigan: William B. Eerdmans Publishing Company, 1978.

Farley, Edward. *Requiem for a Lost Piety: The Contemporary Search for the Chris-tian Life*. Philadelphia: The Westminster Press, 1966.

Fenhagen, James C. *Mutual Ministry: New Vitality for the Local Church*. New York: The Seabury Press—A Crossroad Book, 1977.

Fox, Matthew. *On Becoming a Musical, Mystical Bear: Spirituality American Style*. New York: Paulist Press/Deus Book, 1972.

Gibbs, Mark. *Christians with Secular Power*. Laity Exchange Books. Philadelphia: Fortress Press, 1981.

Gibbs, Mark, and Morton, T. Ralph. *God's Frozen People: A Book For and About Christian Laymen*. Philadelphia: The Westminster Press, 1964.

Glasse, James D. *Putting It Together in the Parish*. Nashville: Abingdon Press, 1972.

Holmes, Urban T., III. *Ministry and Imagination*. New York: The Seabury Press, 1976.

Howe, Reuel L. *Partners in Preaching: Clergy and Laity in Dialogue*. New York: The Seabury Press—A Crossroad Book, 1967.

Hunter, The Rev. George I. "Theological Field Education." Unpublished. Newton Centre, Massachusetts: The Boston Theological Institute, 1977.

Johnson, Robert Clyde, Editor. "The Church and Its Changing Ministry: Study Material Prepared Under the Direction of the General Assembly Special Commit-tee on the Nature of the Ministry, The United Presbyterian Church in the United States of America." Philadelphia: Office of the General Assembly, The United Presbyterian Church in the United States of America, 1961.

Klassen, William. *The Forgiving Community*. Philadelphia: The Westminster Press, 1966.

Kraemer, Hendrik. *A Theology of the Laity.* Philadelphia: The Westminster Press, 1958.

Küng, Hans. *On Being a Christian.* Translated by Edward Quinn. Garden City, New York: Doubleday & Company, Inc., 1976.

Kushner, Harold S. *When Bad Things Happen to Good People.* New York: Schocken Books, 1981.

Leech, Kenneth. *Soul Friend: The Practice of Christian Spirituality.* Introduction by Henri J.M. Nouwen. San Francisco: Harper & Row, 1977.

Levinson, Daniel J., with Darrow, Charlotte N., Klein, Edward B., Levinson, Maria H., and McKee, Braxton. *The Seasons of a Man's Life.* New York: Ballantine Books, 1978.

McCarty, Doran. *The Supervision of Ministry Students.* Atlanta, Georgia: Home Mission Board, Southern Baptist Convention, 1978.

"Minutes, Including Addresses: Thirteenth General Synod, United Church of Christ, Rochester, New York, June 27–July 1, 1981." Edited by Bernice W. Bobo, Ruth Emley, and Joseph H. Evans. New York: Office of the Secretary, The United Church of Christ, 1981.

Moltmann, Jürgen. *The Church in the Power of the Spirit: A Contribution to Messianic Ecclesiology.* Translated by Margaret Kohl. New York: Harper & Row, 1977.

Moltmann, Jürgen. *The Crucified God: The Cross of Christ as the Foundation and Criticism of Christian Theology.* Translated by R.A. Wilson and John Bowden. New York: Harper & Row, 1974.

Moltmann, Jürgen; with Meeks, M. Douglas; Hunter, Rodney J.; Fowler, James W.; and Erskine, Noel L. *Hope for the Church: Moltmann in Dialogue with Practical Theology.* Edited and Translated by Theodore Runyon. Nashville: Abingdon Press, 1979.

Moltmann, Jürgen. *The Passion for Life: A Messianic Lifestyle.* Translated and with an Introduction by M. Douglas Meeks. Philadelphia: Fortress Press, 1978.

Mouw, Richard J. *Called to Holy Worldliness.* Laity Exchange Books. Philadelphia: Fortress Press, 1980.

Nouwen, Henri J.M. *Creative Ministry.* Garden City, New York: Doubleday & Company, Inc., 1971.

Nouwen, Henri J.M. *The Wounded Healer: Ministry in Contemporary Society.* Garden City, New York: Doubleday & Company, Inc., 1972.

Palmer, Parker J. *The Company of Strangers: Christians and the Renewal of America's Public Life.* Foreword by Martin E. Marty. New York: Crossroad, 1981.

Pohly, Kenneth D. *Pastoral Supervision: Inquiries into Pastoral Care, I.* Houston, Texas: The Institute of Religion, Texas Medical Center, 1977.

Pruyser, Paul W. *The Minister as Diagnostician: Personal Problems in Pastoral Perspective.* Philadelphia: The Westminster Press, 1976.

Russell, Letty M. *Growth in Partnership.* Philadelphia: The Westminster Press, 1981.

Russell, Letty M. *The Future of Partnership.* Philadelphia: The Westminster Press, 1979.

Schillebeeckx, Edward. *Jesus: An Experiment in Christology.* Translated by Hubert Hoskins. New York: The Seabury Press—A Crossroad Book, 1979.

Schuller, David S.; Brekke, Milo L.; and Strommen, Merton P.; Assisted by: Galloway, Arlene, and O'Brien, Mary Kay. *Readiness for Ministry: Volume I—Criteria.* Vandalia, Ohio: The Association of Theological Schools in the United States and Canada, 1975.

Smith, Donald P. *Clergy in the Cross Fire: Coping with Role Conflicts in the Ministry.* Philadelphia: The Westminster Press, 1973.

Soelle, Dorothee. *Suffering.* Translated by Everett R. Kalin. Philadelphia: Fortress Press, 1975.

Switzer, David K. *Pastor, Preacher, Person: Developing a Pastoral Ministry in Depth.* Nashville: Abingdon Press, 1979.

Weber, Hans-Ruedi. *Salty Christians.* New York: The Seabury Press, 1963.

Williams, Daniel Day. *The Minister and the Care of Souls.* New York: Harper and Brothers, 1961.